The Self-Help Delusion

A Manifesto For Genuine Change

By

Peter Seal

The Self-Help Delusion © Copyright 2021 by Peter Seal

All rights reserved. No part of this work may be reproduced or stored in an information retrieval system (other than for purposes of review) without prior written permission by the copyright holder.

A catalogue record of this book is available from the British Library

First Edition: March 2021

ISBN: 978-1-84375-628-6

Published by: Prestige Press
Email: info@prestige-press.com
Web: http://www.prestige-press.com

Table of Contents

	Author Profile	7
	Preface	9
	Introduction	13
1.	This Relative World	15
2.	Perception Of Reality	17
3.	The Experience Of Time	23
4.	When Is A Choice	35
5.	The Process Of Changing	47
6.	What Are You?	55
7.	The Creation Of Meaning	65
8.	Communication – General	83
9.	Communication – Tools	99
10.	The Origin Of Belief	109
11.	Criticism And Perfection	117
12.	Judgment And Opinion	127
13.	The Structure Of Love	143
14.	An Analysis Of Responsibility	163
15.	Looking At Trust	169
16.	Ego And Self-Worth	177
17.	Doing Our Happiness	181
18.	Pain And Suffering	191
19.	The Nature Of Emotions	201
20.	Man, God And Religion	217
21.	Personal Spirituality	221
22.	Conclusion	229
23.	Bibliography	231

Author Profile

My background is in science, rather than the arts, and I am an engineer by training and inclination. During my career, I enjoyed a broad range of roles: garage mechanic, college lecturer, shopkeeper, computer programmer, data analyst, product manager and project manager. I spent my final working years on a telephone helpline, supporting employees with personal problems.

Twenty-five years ago, many aspects of my life were not working for me, nor for those around me I suspect. I was full of self-pity, bitterness and frustration, and I was angry at the world and wanted it to change so my problems would be fixed. I had spent many years waiting for that to happen. Needless to say, it never did.

I began to read books on counselling, personal development, psychology, philosophy and spirituality. I became a Master Practitioner of NLP, Hypnosis and Time-Line Therapy. I am also a Qualified Teacher. Gradually, over several years, as my view of myself, the world, and the people around me changed, so too did my internal state.

Thanks to those experiences, finding life tough, and then learning how to have it smoother, I feel well-suited to writing this book. Finally, I had created a sense of wellbeing and contentedness within myself, and I hope this book will enable me to share it with you.

Preface

After many years' experience in the self-help world, I have arrived at the conclusion that the conventional approach to personal change, that of reading and following a conventional self-help book creates little long term behavioral change. A recent survey in The Times showed that only 1% of people starting a diet are still following it a year later; such a lot of effort with no useful outcome.

Those books function by positing a logical argument as why you should change, that indeed you could change, that indeed you ought to change, and that by following the pathway set out in the book, your problem will be solved.

And it may well work, and you may well change.

Then habit and an easier life, and just this once, and I can't be bothered become the drivers of your behavior. Then your old behavior patterns kick in, and within months or less, you are back where you started. Only worse than before because you tried and failed, and you know it's possible but you couldn't do it so there must be something wrong with you.

This is not a good place to be.

There are solid proven psychological reasons why this pattern of behavior is so common.

We behave not from our conscious thoughts but from unconscious patterns and habits. These patterns and habits are formed over a long period of time from our values and our beliefs. Unless we change these, at a non-cognitive level, our new behavior cannot become automatic and habitual, which is necessary for permanent change.

I know a person who has always been overweight; weighing far more that was useful to a long life. A rigorous dieting process was undertaken, and she reduced her weight by nearly 50% over 12 months. She knew what would generate weight loss because weight loss had been achieved; a very successful outcome.

Two years later my friend weighs the same as she did before her diet. She put it all back on again, with concomitant problems with hips and knee joints.

* * * * * * *

This book is about awareness. It's about re-training the unconscious mind to assist us to create new habits that are more useful in enabling us to live the contented life we all crave.

This book does not set out to solve specific problems and there are no exercises to perform on a regular basis. It does not tackle your unwanted behavior head on, as the more energy you give the battle, the more energy the ego and unconscious mind will fight it. It's a subtle change of belief and values which will offer new behaviors to your unconscious mind.

To the reader
This book is perhaps best read from front to back over several sittings, stopping every now and again to ponder what you have read, and its relevance to you. You may then choose to read it again to notice a point missed or rejected the first time through. After that, you may perhaps keep it by your bedside and dip into whenever you feel the need.

The Self-Help Delusion

Believe nothing, O monks, merely because you have been told it... or because it is traditional, or because you yourself have imagined it. Do not believe what your teacher tells you merely out of respect for the teacher.

But whatsoever, after due examination and analysis, you find to be conducive to the good, the benefit, the welfare of all beings - that doctrine believe, and cling to and take as your guide.
Buddha - The Dhammapada

Introduction

What is this life all about?

So many people tell us what life means, what to believe, what to do, how to do it, and what to think whilst doing it.

I'm over seventy years old now, and I believe that I've finally made some sense of it. It took me until now because most things in life do not function in the way that we are led by almost everyone and everything, to believe they do.

As fast as I thought I'd found some acceptable answers, something or someone happened in my life, causing me to re-think my ideas and beliefs about life, love and the pursuit of happiness.

When I was younger, I followed the well trodden path to contentedness by looking for 'The Truth'. The problem is that if you go outside of yourself for the truth, the truth you get will depend on who you ask. The only truth that can really matter to you and provide your contentedness is your truth.

Socrates is credited with the expression, 'The unexamined life is not worth living'. This book is an invitation to examine various beliefs, behaviors and the choices you are making each day as you live your life.

I've subtitled the book 'A Manifesto for Genuine Change' because generally, self-help books aim to solve some perceived problem in your life. As in 'this book will change your life' and make you slimmer, richer, happier, more attractive, sexier, irresistible, calmer etc. And they all tell you the truth.

Much in this book is quite provocative in its directness, but it doesn't tell you the truth. It does however hold a series of alternative thoughts about the way you can live your life, because many of the beliefs that got us to where we are now will not optimally allow us to move on to the next phase of our lives, whatever we decide that to be.

And the magical thing is that when you change your beliefs about yourself and the world and become aware of yourself, what you really are, what you are really doing here, problems you thought you had will disappear without any conscious effort. You will suddenly notice that you don't do those problems anymore, because you don't have to.

Whatever problem you did will simply become an option which you now no longer need to choose.

* * * * * * *

You see Doctor, it hurts when I do this.
Do the words 'stop doing it' mean anything to you?

This Relative World

I'm starting off with the premise that this world is a relative world and full of comparisons. Given your current thinking, this piece may seem irrelevant but later on you will hopefully appreciate its significance.

People usually associate relativity with Einstein and quantum mechanics but here we are not concerned with that aspect.

This is a relative world. As an example: Take up and down. 'Up' is relative to 'Down'. Down is where the earth is, and up is where the sky is. That's obvious, but if we ask the astronauts in space, the earth is only 'Down' and the sky 'Up' relative to where we are when we use the words. These words have no meaning in space unless the astronauts decide that looking down is when they look at the earth. As they get closer to the moon, the moon suddenly becomes a far more significant 'down' than the earth which is over 230,000 miles away. Up and down are relative to each other, opposite to each other in fact, but have no specific meaning outside of the context in which they are used. They are relative both to themselves and to everything else. Without down, there can be no up, and vice-verse. To extend this idea, without a left, there is no right, without little there can be no big, without slow there can be no fast etc. This also applies to moral judgments, without bad, there can be no good, without wrong, there can be no right; our entire world is relative, populated by opposites.

Sometimes one aspect is compared to a thought that we have. 'Oh, I expected him to be older than he is'. Older compared to what? Older is a comparative word, and the other half of the comparison is in your head. Nothing stands in isolation. And here is an important point. Many of the 'relative to' comparisons that we make are simply just ideas in our heads. All of your judgments come from comparing reality as you 'see' it against the way you think it should be. Sometimes the world is better than your expectations, and sometimes worse. I suspect generally worse.

Movement is always relative. Think about when you are sitting on a train temporarily stationary in the station. As you look out of the nearest window, you see another train on the adjacent track. Suddenly, it begins to move slowly in the opposite direction to the one your carriage was traveling. How do you process that event? What's happening at this point? Without looking for something not moving, you cannot know. Is it moving away from you, or are you moving away from it?

Another, perhaps a little less obvious example: in English we call the sky 'blue'. We look up – sometimes – to a blue sky. But the sky is not blue.

What is happening is that your eye detects light from the sky. Your brain can differentiate one wavelength of light from another, and the message sent to the brain we call blue. In reality the sky isn't blue. Your brain processes the sensations it receives from your eyes and we call the resultant sensation blue. It is the sensation that we call blue, not the sky. The sky itself has no colour. Colour does not exist without a human to give it a name.

Does the sky look blue to a colour blind person?

The important realisation is that you are the blue, not the sky. You are creating the blue in your head. At this point, I can imagine you thinking – so what – but just hold the thought. It will be essential later.

Perception of Reality

"Reality is merely an illusion, albeit a very persistent one." - Albert Einstein (1879-1955)

"Reality is that which, when you stop believing in it, doesn't go away." Philip K Dick

To follow on and broaden the horizon a little further, let's think about Reality - what is real, and what is not. The word 'real' has several meanings and it is used to mean different things in different contexts. For me, a thing is 'real' when it takes up space in our reality. anything else is a matter of opinion, and that is 'that which appears real' as opposed to that created by the imagination.

Which begs the questions - appears real to whom, and created by whose imagination, and does the same 'that' which appears real to me appear real to you or any other person - to all others even? And do we share the same creations of individual imaginations, and thus share the same delusions of reality? And have we, as human beings perhaps been programmed by the evolutionary process to have the same delusions about reality?

The problems come when people decide that their reality is the only reality, and any other 'real' is the figment of another's imagination and isn't really real. The trick to realise is that your real is a figment of your imagination and isn't real either. There is no 'real' other than that which we are creating in our head.

That can seem nonsense. A chair is 'real', that table is 'real'. They are not figments of our imagination. But don't forget that we perhaps agreed that the colour blue was created in your head.

For me, an object is real if it takes up space in the world – ignoring quantum mechanics for the moment.

Some things are obviously what they seem to be and have obvious characteristics. In our niche of the world, a chair is obviously a chair, and a table, a table. Let's take something that is in common use – say your computer. It is real, in that it takes up space and we can agree that it is solid in that it would make a crash if we dropped it on the floor.

However, nuclear physics tells us that it isn't solid. In the physicist's very practical world, all the components which make up the computer are in their turn made up of atoms, each with a nucleus, and electrons spinning round some relative distance away. There is no 'matter' holding the electrons in their orbits, in the same way that there is no matter holding the earth and the planets in their orbits as they rotate around the sun – though not for the same reason. That space isn't solid and the space in the atom isn't solid either.

In common use, the computer is solid, but it is also 'full' of space. It can be either of these things at the same time.

I think we generally make the mistake of using the conjunction 'or' rather than 'and'. Think of it as both solid and not solid. It all depends on how you choose to look at it, how much you know, and which view allows you to investigate the characteristics that you are interested in.

The atomic physicist is interested in the computer as made of atoms with a nucleus and electrons (and all manner of sub atomic particles).

The chemical engineer is interested in the computer as having plastic components made of oxygen (a gas) and hydrogen (another gas) combined together in chemical bonds of long chain polymers (plastic), together with the steel, copper, silver and glass and numerous other elements and compounds forming the electronic components.

You are interested in the computer as a tool maybe for work, leisure and communication.

These three views of the computer: atomic, chemical and functional are all valid, all true – all real. Each provides an accurate and viable way to think of your computer. But they are complimentary views, not exclusive views, and taken together, provides us with three different aspects, different realities, of the same object.

The point is that it is our senses and our brain that creates our personal sense of reality, and that our sense of reality can, indeed will change if we change our vantage point and our desired outcomes.

Without your senses, you would have a very different reality. If you had no sight, touch, feel, smell or taste, your understanding of what was 'real' would change totally. You would not exist relative to another. You would be in total isolation in this world; your thought processes perhaps without words, your body without feeling, your ears without sound etc.

To all intents and purposes, you would not exist in this world. Or to be more exact, the world would not exist in you, certainly not the world as you now know it. You could be experienced by others who had their full set of faculties, but you could not experience them. In fact, you could not even experience yourself.

That will be obvious if you agreed earlier that everything we experience is relative to something else. Whatever your experiences would be in that situation, there would be nothing to which they could be related. How would you know yourself if there was nothing your experiences could be related to? If you could create any sort of reality – and that's doubtful, it could only be inside your head.

If you were suddenly placed in an isolation tank, you would still be able to think and re-live your memories, but within a few hours, many people have a real problem with holding their identity. They start to lose touch with themselves, and when brought out, they are very confused for several hours.

That's one reason why prisoners are held in solitary confinement. They have their full senses, sight, hearing, smell etc. but only within the confines of their cell and psychologically, that is very disturbing.

It is only through our senses that we can know the world exists, and the stimuli they provide to the brain are interpreted in the brain. In this respect, your reality only exists in your brain. It is created in your head and it exists in your head, for where else could it exist? Is it in a flower, or a daughter, or a wife, or a job? Perhaps it's simply everywhere.

Problem is, you only know about 'everywhere' through your senses, and your interpretation of the signals that your senses present to your brain.

Reality – your interpretation of 'everywhere' - happens inside your head, as it does for a bee, seeking out the flowers with the most pollen, or a bat, 'seeing' the world at night by the radar squeaks it makes, and the dog, running with his nose close to the ground, creating the reality of another animal who passed by recently.

You go outside, and you are bombarded by radio signals, mobile phone signals, thousands of waves moving past you and through you. A human being has no means of realising that (making them real) unless they carry a radio, a mobile phone and a television set. Our bodies and brains have no way of including them in our reality, because we don't have the sense mechanism to detect and interpret them. But cognitively, we know they are undoubtedly there.

I say again, you create your reality in your head, for there's nowhere else for it to exist. Our human reality is what our brain creates from the sensory experiences that we have, combined with our memory of what has already happened to us and the expectations of what might happen to us in the future. This automatically makes one person's reality different to another's.

A friend of mine suffered (still does to some extent) from psychosis. She wrote a book (unpublished) which she titled 'The Illusion of Reality from inside a Psychotic Mind'. Hers was a very different reality at that time, which later, in recovery, she realised that she had been creating in her mind. Her reality was as real to her as mine is to me and yours is to you.

I am saying that we create our reality behind our eyes, not in front of them, in our head rather than in our experiencing reality out there and then taking it into our mind as though it were a fixed entity. Reality is not a fixed entity that you detect and live within. You are creating it as you go along, and we all create it differently.

This may be an enormous shift in your understanding, as it is for most people, because nothing in our every-day world suggests that it is like that.

Most people live and die and never realise that they are creating their own reality; that indeed, everything 'out there' is actually created 'in here'.

When you see these things, you can realise that you always have a choice as to how you 'see' things, and that the way you see them is no more or less valid than the different ways other people see them. In order for your world to change and be more in keeping to the way you wish it to be, you have to change your thoughts and the words you use to describe those thoughts. Then the world you create in your head will better serve your life and your love and your pursuit of happiness.

People spend most of their time telling everyone else that their way is the real way, and that everyone else is wrong.

All I aim to do is to awaken you to the realisation that there is a choice in the way you see reality and that choice it is a massively powerful tool to assist you in growing your life.

The Experience of Time

The Moving Finger writes; and, having writ,
Moves on: nor all thy Piety nor Wit
Shall lure it back to cancel half a Line,
Nor all thy Tears wash out a Word of it.

Rubaiyat of Omar Khayyam

Time is the major controlling factor in our lives, and one we cannot do much about.

In this world, the speed of time seems to be constant and that it controls the existence of past, present and future in the 'real' world. This is the way the 'reality' of time has always been perceived, and the one we need in order to function in this world.

On the other hand, there is the space / time continuum, where space and time are interlinked. When the space between two objects is changing, the speed of time on one object, when measured from the other, is reduced. It's as though when the space between the objects is changing, the speed of time decreases to maintain a balance. Einstein perceived this 'reality' of time

Thinking on another level, time does not exist as we perceive it and is a man-made construction. Spiritualists, philosophers and quantum physicists acknowledge this 'reality' of time. There is only 'now', and time, as we conceive it, cannot exist in the moment of now. This moment of 'Now' does not have a past or a future.

These realisations make time just as 'relative' as everything else. It depends on how we look at it, and where we are coming from. Time is a curious process. We - mankind - we split time up into the three divisions of past, present and future, and then believe them all to be real. At least we behave as though we believed them to be real (remember my definition of real – does it take up space in the world). We need to do this to function in this relative existence. We have spent all our life making these thoughts real, that to think otherwise requires a large shift in perception. Bear with me and let's look in a very simple way at how realistic these beliefs are, and how useful it is perhaps to realise time in another way.

I will use the word 'realise' many times in my writings, and generally I want you to give it the meaning 'to make real' – as in your thoughts or your imagination, your language and your actions.

Looking at what we mean by time and the way we think of it at the moment.

Take the past. What is real about the past? Think about your relationship with a friend. This relationship does not exist in universal reality in that it cannot be experienced by other than the people involved (as opposed to the Eiffel tower which can). It only exists in your memory, and in the memory of your friend, and sometimes your memory of that relationship does not match that of your friend. Because of your shared memories, you believe that since you feel a particular way about what happened, they must feel the same way too. I mean, how could they not? We are both part of the same relationship are we not?

But it doesn't work that way. We are often so wrapped up in how we want the relationship to be, but my friend may not remember the past in the same way that I believe they must, and they don't respond in the way I want them to and that can hurt.

If we had no long-term memory, we would not have the sensation of long term relationships. Everyone and everything would be of this moment; each moment being created anew, without reference to the past and without our feelings carried forward from that past. In some cases, the longings and / or fears remembered of the happenings in the past colour what we do and think today. None of that would exist if we had no long-term memory and we could live each day as a new fresh day. It's our memory that provides us with the impression that the past is real.

But the past is not real, and it has no existence outside of our personal reality of memory. The past did exist. Past tense; and it was Now when it existed. It must have existed for you to have memories of it, but it doesn't exist now. Of course, events in the past have changed things, the Big Bang to create the universe, evolution of life on earth, evolution of mankind etc to mention only the little things. This is not to say that the past didn't exist, of course it did; it just doesn't now.

When we argue with our friend about the shared past experiences, we argue about our memory and our remembering of that memory as against their memory of the same event. As we will see later, we only recall those things that make sense or are considered necessary in our reality at the time the memory was laid down. We don't remember the totality of what happened, or if we do, we don't recall it and act on it. We inevitably filter out much of the actual event.

The mind has to filter out some of the data that our five senses provide; 1000's of bits of data at every moment. These bits of data are passed to the unconscious mind. We cannot possibly cognitively process all this data, so it is filtered through our unconscious mind and only that which is considered of interest is passed into consciousness, at which point, by adding a meaning, we turn it into information. There is considerable evidence that we store it all, we just don't process it all.

You can only be cognitively aware of a very small portion of the data that is coming into your mind from the outside world.

To support this thought, can you feel your left foot in your shoe?

Now you can, but you didn't until my words directed your attention to your foot. Your unconscious mind simply decided that that data was not of any significance and deleted it.

When we remember things, we only remember, or more significantly, we can only consciously recall, that which we were interested in at the time when we laid down the memory and our conscious recall is very selective.

Under hypnosis, a person can be helped to recall a great deal more about an event but that of course can be dangerous because people can be 'helped to recall' events that never occurred.

Under hypnosis, the unconscious mind is available, and it is very susceptible to suggestion. One of the characteristics of the unconscious mind is that it wants to please, and the unconscious is desperately looking for a reason why it feels the way it does. Any possibility offered by the practitioner is clutched on as being the truth. Many problems have been created by hypnotists who didn't know what they were doing, or were so besotted by a theory, that they were going to have it validated, one way or another; unconsciously besotted of course.

We also filter the messages that come in through our senses by generalising them. We even generalise about opening doors. Any door with a round handle you would expect to rotate the handle and pull or push the door to open it. We have one at home which slides, and everybody tries to push it open.

It is this process of generalisation that produces racism. It's easy to generalise that all Germans are methodical and followers of orders, and all Americans are loud mouths, and all Italians wave their hands around. These may be seen as national characteristics, and we often generalise in order to process the information that comes to us. However, we need to be very conscious that we are creating a general reality which may in fact not be specifically true about this German or this American or this Italian.

What you remember about the past is uniquely yours, since you can only consciously recall and give meaning to a subset of the data that was available at the time? Your unconscious mind did not pass it on to your conscious mind. It was not deleted completely, as your unconscious mind still knows it.

Tests have been done where parts of the brain of a patient were stimulated by small electrical currents. The patient had total recall of an event stored in the area stimulated but otherwise forgotten. It's like they are living the experience again. When the stimulus is removed, the experience stops.

And here's the amazing thing, when the stimulus is re-applied, the experience begins again, but not from when where it was when the stimulus stopped, but from the beginning of the experience. And we can only conjecture as to why. It's a bit like the repeat option on a video recorder. The data is in the mental memory and all we have to do is to stimulate the correct part to set it playing again.

The above has us realise that often what you believe about an event in the past didn't happen, or at least, didn't happen the way you can consciously recall it. Well, what you believe happened did happen, from your point of view, and from the state of your mind at the time. The data from your senses was 'censored' by your unconscious mind and passed to your conscious mind where you created your meaning. In creating meaning - changing data into information - there was some deletion, distortion and some generalisation taking place. The event as you remember it is the output from that process. Of course, we don't think like that, all these processes happening in moments, but it's a useful model which seems to explain the results of countless academic studies.

These realisations of course allow us to be a lot less critical about what others say, and much less sure of what we say. There is no point arguing at length over past history. We each believe that the way we remember it is the way it was. And it is as far as we know. We believe it to be true, but, to quote the old song, "It ain't necessarily so".

What you remember about the past is uniquely yours, since you can only consciously recall and give meaning to a subset of the data that you became consciously aware of at the time. When it's put like that, arguing over the past seems such a waste of time, but how we fight to be believed, because we know that what we believe - our version of the past - is the correct one, and indeed the only one and everyone else is wrong.

Now I realise this, I no longer fight for my memory of a past event to be accepted as the right remembrance of the past. Being 'right' is not important unless you're in a quiz game, and life is not a quiz game, and our relationships are often irreparably damaged by needing to have our 'reality' of the past accepted by another.

It seems to me that mankind is be-devilled with memories of history. History is the reason, or the excuse, for pretty much any sort of behavior. Take somewhere close to home - Northern Ireland. Until recently, events some three hundred years ago were still causing death and pain. One side celebrates a victory – and has the legal right to do but they do so in a way calculated to antagonise the other side. 'We have the right' they say, forgetting that in a civilised society, they also have the obligation to exercise that right in a responsible way. Looking in from the outside, it is pathetic and childish. But history, and sectarianism, and pride, and religion and vengeance, and 'rights' and 'the force of history' are so entrenched in the people's hearts that they cannot let it go.

The sad thing is that they are going nowhere until they do let it go. The past does not exist. It is not real. Study it, learn from it, and then let it go and move into the here and now.

* * * * * * *

We believe we see life as a continually changing picture. Think of going to the cinema. The picture appears to be moving. In fact, it isn't. It is just a series of still pictures - frames - presented to the eyes frequently enough to have the brain believe it to be moving.

When a frame has been seen, it is history, and we cannot experience it again. When a frame is just about to be seen, it is the future, and we do not know what it will look like - though we can take a good guess. 'Now' is the frame on the screen in that split $1/26^{th}$ of a second - less in fact, as there is time passing between the changing of the frames as we see them.

Life is a series of 'now' presented very rapidly but in each frame, we see - for a short period of time - there is no past and no future. There is only the frame we see 'now'.

That's the best metaphor I can come up with to describe a process which we live inside. We have to get outside it to really 'see' it, and until death, we cannot do that.

To support my thoughts, I came across a book called 'Permanent Present Tense'. When he was twenty-seven, Henry Molaison underwent surgery for his epilepsy. He awoke with part of his brain destroyed, and for the rest of his life would be trapped in the moment, unable to remember anything for more than a few seconds. For nearly five decades, distinguished neuroscientist Suzanne Corkin studied Molaison and oversaw his care. In her book, she tells his extraordinary story, showing how his amnesia revolutionised our understanding of the brain, and also challenged our very notions of who we are. For him, time as we know it did not exist.

Clive Wearing suffers from anterograde amnesia (meaning he can't create new memories) as well as retrograde amnesia (meaning he's lost many of his memories). For him, life is a haze somewhere between consciousness and slumber. His memories from his life before 1985 are very few. Wearing contracted a herpes virus that attacks the nervous system. The effects of the illness were so great that, now, he lacks the ability to form new memories, and he also cannot recall aspects of his past memories. According to his wife, his memory lasts between 7 and 30 seconds. Every day, he feels that he's "waking up" several times a minute, as his consciousness is essentially rebooting. Indeed, it is said that he recurrently believes that he has just woken from a coma.

We create time in our heads, as indeed we create everything else.

* * * * * * * *

The future isn't real either. We create it in our minds whenever we want to; sometimes even when we don't want to. If we are anxious, we are anxious not for what is happening now, because we are coping with that, but for what might happen to us in the future. All anxiety is a fear of the future. Obviously, in many cases this can be useful. We could find ourselves in serious danger if we did not use our experience - our remembered interpretation of a past 'reality', to influence our behavior and warn against a particular course of action that caused pain the last time we did it.

I was sitting on the train recently, and, when it poured with rain, and since the train was old, water was leaking in round the windows. There was a group of people sitting around me who were complaining about the rain, and how even if it were fine now, it would be raining when they got to our station down the line. "You wait, it'll be pouring with rain when we get to our station, it always is" said one. "No sooner have we opened the train doors it will be raining" said another. They all in unison agreed that that was very likely to be the case. They spent ten minutes bewailing the 'fact' that it would be raining when they left the train, and the size of the puddles in the car park, and how they would be wet and cold when they got home, and how terrible it would all be.

And I thought to myself. Here are four intelligent normal people creating in their minds a future that none of them want, and about which they can do nothing, and then they spend the next ten minutes complaining and feeling bad about it. That's got to be crazy. If it is going to be raining, it will be raining, and if not, then not. There was nothing they could do about it and no additional precautions they could take.

As it happened, it was overcast, but hadn't rained there all day.

This approach can cause anxiety and worry about a future event that may very well not occur, and that you can cope with even if it does. It also inhibits our spontaneity and our taking of chances.

All of our anxiety comes from creating an unpleasant future in our minds and making it real now. I remember traveling to work, again on the train one morning a few months ago. I was completely relaxed after reading some esoteric tome about Life, God and the Universe. Totally chilled, and at peace with the world. Then I thought about the work I would be involved in when I reached the office. I had a deadline to make, very important to the company, and at that time, to me as well. I should have sorted it by now. What if the muse doesn't strike and I can't fulfill my obligation. My manager will be breathing fire, I will be embarrassed, and … and…. within 20 seconds I was feeling decidedly warm, started to sweat, I could feel my heart beginning to pound and my breathing beginning to shorten. All the classic signs of anxiety began to set in. Until I realised what I was doing to myself, what my mind was doing. Once realised, and that there was nothing I could do about the situation sitting on the train, I consciously changed my thoughts to the then and there to restore my emotional equilibrium. There was no atmosphere of fear present on the train, nobody around me threatened me. I did it all myself, with my little mind, I made me scared. The day passed as all days do, I completed my work on time, and everybody was happy.

The Self-Help Delusion

If we have to create a fantasy future in our heads, then let's at least create a pleasant one, not one where all the things that can go wrong do go wrong. Consider them, plan for them, but don't live in them.

Most people suffer from anxiety and whatever the content of the anxiety, it will be some time in the future. I mean, you can't be anxious about the past can you. That's already happened, and you survived it. You may have many feelings about the past, but anxiety won't be one of them.

I realise that it's easier read about than done, but when you find yourself becoming anxious next time, realise what you are doing and change your thoughts, direct your attention someplace else.

There is no future in it – if you'll pardon the pun – and all you do is to get yourself upset unnecessarily. And anxiety does not accompany a peaceful mind. Hopefully, by the time we have finished this book you will find it easier to leave the future to look after itself.

Let's now look at the third area in man's construction of time; the present.

The present is the only time there is. That's now, right now, and now, now, now, now, and as each now disappears into the past, it is not a now, and becomes only a memory. That now no longer exists. Only now exists, and now has no time, because if it had, there could be no now because the now in time is instantly replaced by another now. Time cannot exist in the now. And now is all we have. We experience a continuous and uninterrupted now. There are no past nows, and there can be no future nows.

I am saying that there is no real past, and no real future, and 'now' cannot exist in time either, as 'now' has been replaced by another 'now' in the instant that I realise it is 'now'.

I believe we need reminding every so often about 'now' as most of us do not live with that idea in our behavior. If we did, we wouldn't spend half our time thinking about the past, and the other half thinking about the future. If we are lucky, we spend about 5% of our time in the 'now'. The problem is that we cannot do anything in the past, it has already happened, and we cannot do anything in the future. When we do whatever we have planned for the future, it is 'now' when we do them. But this 'now' was the future when we planned it. We can only ever do things in the 'now'. This is not to say that we shouldn't learn from the past, or plan for the future, but we should be very aware when we are doing these things, and not try and correct what we did in the past with remorse and guilt or fantasies an unpleasant future that may very well not happen. Or even fantasise a pleasant future for too long. Moments spent this way can be enjoyable of course, and that's fine. But be aware, the only moment you can live is now.

Now' is accessed by leaving the mind and getting into your senses and feelings.

Here is an exercise to help you get to 'now'.

Your senses can only tell you what is happening here and now. You cannot sense the past or the future without some part of your mind going there first. You can remember sensations from the past, but you cannot experience them in the past. All sensations and emotions are created in the now.

Sit in a comfortable position. Do it now; don't just read this. Do it!

Shift your attention to all the feelings that you are receiving from the real world. Feel the chair under you, the back of the chair against your back; the feel of the floor under your feet, and the feel of your socks against your skin, then the feel of your hands touching the book or reader.

Live with those feelings for a time. Only the now has feelings.

Shift your attention to the signals reaching your ears, to the sounds around you.

Listen to the silences between the sounds.

Create no comments in your mind about the sounds.

Put no names to the sounds; make no judgments as to the nature of the sounds. Sound is sound is sound. It is neither good nor bad. What you feel about it is a judgment and a statement about how your history and your evolution are inviting you to feel about it. It says nothing about the sound itself. There are no harsh sounds. There are no sweet sounds, there are no ugly sounds, and

The Self-Help Delusion

there are no beautiful sounds. Only sounds. And what you make of the sound, the feeling that you attach to that sound is the way you come to describe it. The sound itself has no meaning. Listen to the background noises, the lorry going past or the birds in the trees or the children playing and laughing or your partner talking to someone else on the phone; whatever. Listen to all those sounds, put your attention to them, all those sounds, to each specifically, and then as a totality of sound. Only the now has sounds.

Sense the taste in your mouth, the taste of your saliva, the taste of the tea you've just drunk, or the breakfast you have just had, or the cigarette you have just smoked. The taste you still have in your mouth. Saver those tastes, for they are real. You can only taste in the now. The past has no taste, the future has no taste; you might remember the taste of something in the past, but it is a memory, and you may anticipate a taste you might experience in the future, but that is a taste you create in your imagination and it too comes from your memory. Taste can only be experienced now. Only the now has a taste.

Open your eyes to what you can see. Cast your eyes over whatever is in front of you. See it as though it is a picture in a frame. It is neither ugly nor beautiful. It just is. You, in your own mind, you make it beautiful or you make it ugly or you make it unremarkable. And we generally do just that. We make unremarkable everything that isn't special, and we make special only that which we have learned to consider special. Make no judgments. There is no beauty without mankind to associate to that beauty. There is no ugliness, only mankind to associate it to something that isn't wanted. For ugliness and beauty do not exist outside of the human mind, nor do the judgments that our minds persist in making about everything. Everything just is; it is real. The past cannot be seen. The future cannot be seen.

Only the now can be seen.

Go through your senses like this; first one at a time, and then from one to the other in succession.

* * * * * * * *

This exercise will help to reduce stress and to be relaxed. When you go to your senses, the problems and pressures of the day disappear for two good reasons.

Problems and pressures cannot exist in the now: they can only exist in the past – recent perhaps, or the future – imminent perhaps, but they cannot exist in the now.

They are created as a result of what has just happened – the past or what you think is going to happen – the future. The moment of now has no problems and pressures.

Sometimes it takes a while to concentrate the mind on the sensations being received through the senses. Whilst you are doing this, the mind cannot be working on the things causing you stress. There was a famous piece of research done some time ago that concluded that the mind can only hold or operate on a limited number of items at any one time; somewhere between five and nine. This is described as 7+/-2. We have 5 senses and putting our attention on them takes up a large proportion of the mind's processing space. Incidentally, because of 7 +/- 2 we remember telephone numbers by 'chunking' them. To remember 01276438560 we generally chunk it like 01276, 438, 560 or 0127, 643, 8560

So, in order to relieve the trials and tribulations of your day, take a short trip to your senses. Visit the now by accessing all the feelings that your senses, your connections to this reality, can experience, and this will push the troubles of the day out of your mind.

When is a Choice

As long as anyone believes that his ideal and purpose is outside him, that it is above the clouds, in the past or in the future, he will go outside himself and seek fulfillment where it cannot be found. He will look for solutions and answers at every point except where they can be found--in himself.
Erich Fromm

I think that the next series of your beliefs to review are those around choice. What constitutes real choice in your life?

I believe that every thought, word, and deed comes about as the result of a choice; either a conscious choice taken now or an unconscious choice taken now or some time earlier in our life and never re-evaluated.

Some time ago, I was working in a multi-cultural office, and I was complaining about something and used the expression 'problem is, there are too many chiefs, and not enough Indians in this company'. The more I tried to explain, the deeper the hole I dug. I acquired that expression when I was a child; we did not give a thought to racism in those days and it was totally acceptable then. I didn't make any decision to say it or not say it, it's just a figure of speech which I'd never questioned – until then. Needless to say, I've deleted it from my phrase bank in case a sensitive person might think me racist.

We process choice at various levels within our mind/body. I call them levels because it seems to me that amateur psychobabble really doesn't help in understanding, but a simple metaphor might. (All psychobabble in any case is no more than a formally agreed series of metaphors or models that are given complex names.)

In order to understand what I'm calling levels, perhaps now is the time for me to introduce the model of the human being as used by NLP.

NLP is an acronym for Neuro Linguistic Programming. It has a number of techniques centered on a series of beliefs about how human beings operate in this world. Originated in the USA in the early seventies and created as a tool in therapy, it has been taken up by industry as being a most effective model in training, motivating and changing the behaviors of employees, from the MD or CEO downwards. It covers a vast field, but at this point, I only want to look at one aspect, the model of the human being used in NLP. It's 'a' model, notice, not 'the' model, but like all models, it provides a tool to better understand or explain the object or process being modeled. In this case it's useful to be able to visualise the relationships between the levels of a human being.

In this model, we consist of three parts:

The body
The conscious mind
The unconscious mind

In this model we have three aspects, but they are aspects of one entity; a little like the Christian model of God - Father, Son, and Holy Spirit. Three aspects, yet all one bound together. No one part functions alone; in this world at any rate.

> The **Body** the function of which is obvious; it gives us physical presence in the world and at least five senses to create a physical awareness of our body and of the world.

> The **Conscious Mind** is that part of our mind that is aware and does the thinking, and makes our decisions more rational (we hope.).

> The **Unconscious Mind** is that part of us which holds our memories, our fears, our inhibitions, our beliefs, our habits,

our emotions and our strategies and also controls the maintenance of our body.

I've included another point, the **Higher Self** – Soul – some would call it, which is that aspect of us that does not die when the other three aspects of our earthly existence do. This is not part of the NLP model but it works for me. You can take it or leave it as your current belief system determines.

The NLP model provides a basis for the forms of internal communication within us.

If we take the mind and the body as one, which I realise is a very broad statement, but let's just accept it as true for the moment. There are several 'presuppositions' which form the core of NLP, which are not in any way proved to be true, but if just accepted as true, they will lead to more useful behaviors than if we argue over them. You see, I'm not looking for the truth, I'm looking for what works. It's easy to argue over truth, more difficult to argue over what works, so consider the mind and the body to be one. The level above is the unconscious mind, and communication is constantly passing between the conscious mind / body and the unconscious mind. The unconscious mind also communicates with the higher self and vice-versa, but more of that later.

Let's take the lowest level of activity first. This is the re-action that the body makes without the mind thinking about it even for one split second. It fact, some argue that in an emergency the message never even reaches the mind and the mind can be surprised by what the body has done. What we call an instinctive re-action. When we trip up, we put our hands out in front of us to protect our vulnerable parts – our face and stomach, and there's not a lot of conscious thought about the action. On one occasion, I was going to work through London Bridge station. I slipped on the wet platform, and suddenly found myself on the floor. I had no time to do anything. A lady said, 'are you hurt'. I said, 'only my dignity'. I didn't have time to decide on the way down, should I put my hands out or should I not bother.

If you just stumble you may have time to anticipate the fall and you do have time to think what to do on the way down. I remember stumbling on a broad mountain path once, and I clearly remember tucking my head into my chest, doing a forward roll and my only injury was a cut on my hand.

When we pick up a very hot coal or pan or something without realising that it is hot, we drop it immediately. There is no time to think about it. The body realises that it is being damaged, and self preservation causes it to act without thought.

If the item is not quite so hot, and has great value to us, the mind seems to make a choice of, do I drop it, and maybe break it, or do I put it down gently, and suffer the pain a little longer. At that point, the conscious mind has become involved in the process, and is in a position to make a decision.

Recently my wife was cooking dinner and the roast potatoes needed turning. I took the oven glove, opened the oven door, but could only hold one end of the heavy cast iron casserole dish. It was half way out of the oven when I realised that because of the pressure on my thumb, the heat was coming through the old glove. I had time, rapidly, to set it on the floor without spilling any of the fat or loosing the potatoes. I didn't want to drop it as that would have been part of dinner spoiled. Even though the action burnt my thumb more than it would have had I dropped it, I decided not to.

The unconscious mind makes decisions too. One of the problems that some people have is the instinctive urge to retaliate in the presence of a perceived threat. They lash out first, either verbally or in some cases physically and then regret what they have done. This is the flash of anger that comes from fear of attack at one level or another. The fear message often doesn't even get as far as the conscious mind. It is pure reaction, like dropping a hot coal, and the stimulus is rather similar too, except that the threat may not be a physical one, only an emotional one. An attack to the ego, or self respect, to dignity or reputation or pride can be perceived by the unconscious mind as just as much an attack. Some will try to justify their anger and their actions because they still feel vulnerable, but others realise immediately that they have broken societies' and their own code of ethics, and apologise.

It is difficult to change that re-action because it comes from

The Self-Help Delusion

the unconscious mind and is created by a belief. It never gets to the conscious mind where a decision can be made about how to respond to the perceived threat to the ego, self respects, dignity, reputation or pride. These are all aspects of the way we define ourselves to ourselves, and it is necessary to change these aspects of self-definition so that the conscious mind has time to intervene.

When you create the belief or realisation that re-acting in an aggressive or habitual way is likely to lose you something of value, the unconscious mind will pass the message to the conscious mind and a rational decision can be made to create a useful response appropriate to the situation.

For example, say you have a friend whom you have known for years. You get on well, and although different in many ways, there is a mutual affection and a mutual respect for each other's differences. But this morning, he is generally feeling out of sorts with the world, and some of his negative demeanor influences his normally acceptable conversation. What do you do when he begins criticising your mother? Inevitably you can feel yourself becoming angry as your loyalty to your mother is being put to the test. Now you definitely have the time to choose your response. How do you respond to the stimulus of your friend's comments?

If you snap off a re-action from the unconscious mind with something like, "Look, shut up about my mother will you. All you ever do these days is slag off my family, just because my family have money and yours doesn't and you can't get over your jealousy". Your relationship will be changed, and you will have made a withdrawal from the bank of goodwill you have with him. If you keep on re-acting in similar ways, you will loose that friend.

Far better to say something like: "Yes, I can see why you might see it that way, but let's move on. What have you planned for the weekend." or "God Tony, you are pissed off this morning (with a laugh), what's bugging you. It isn't Joanna again is it?" or something similar which suits your style. The result then is at worst a change of subject, and at best a coming together as he feels free to tell you the real reason for his frustrations, and an acceptance that your mother isn't really the reason, she's just one of several, and he choose that one because of the association with you.

A favorite quote of mine is: Between stimulus and response, there is a space, and in that space, you have the power to choose your response, and in that choice lays your freedom and your future.

The trick seems to lie in the awareness of the choice we make to generate our response to the stimuli, and to lift the place where that choice is made from the unconscious mind - an automatic habitual re-action - to a consciously considered response. Over a period of time, that consciously chosen response becomes an unconscious habitual one and that will better serve you and provide you with an opportunity for growth.

This is all very well I hear you saying, 'but it will take for ever to change my habitual responses to things.' True, but ask yourself now, in the consciousness of awareness, what do you loose by flashes of anger, either verbal or physical? Not what do you gain from them, because your ego will always justify its actions, but what will you loose? What have you already lost by this behavior?

By creating more choices in the way, you respond to events in your life, you will improve the quality of your relationships, both with others and with yourself. And we often do not realise that it is the relationship you have with yourself that is the most important relationship in your life; because wherever you go, and whoever you go with, you will always be there.

You will change as a result of these additional choices that you are now giving yourself. You will change because when you choose a response to a stimulus, you become, over a period of time, that which you have chosen to be. To quote: "By your actions are you thus defined", and you will become the sort of person who does that sort of actions.

I figuratively, if not often literally, help old ladies across the road because that action is representative of the person I choose to be. Likewise, I do not get into fights in pubs because that is not representative of the person I choose to be. When you have determined who you wish to be, act in sympathy with that image. Then the image will be you and you will become that person.

The first step to change is to determine who you want to be in this world, and then act as that person would act. Can it be that simple?

Yes, it is that simple. But there is a big difference between simple and easy. In practice, it isn't easy because we are all victims of our unconscious re-actions - habits that we have learned over our history, and they are hard taskmasters.

Many people would say that it is maybe our nature to be the way we are, and of course, it is. Some even believe that it's not possible to change their nature - its God given - or some such thought. The problem is that if you believe that, you are absolutely right, it is impossible to change your nature.

If, however you believe that, in the process of living your life, decision by decision, you have chosen your nature then you can also believe that you can re-choose it. In fact, every decision you make about your behavior either confirms or changes your 'nature'.

Note, I'm not saying that simply thinking it to be true makes it true. The world does not change by your thinking it should, and you won't either. The bottom line is that what you believe, not just think, changes your behavior. If you believe you are a fixed entity, then you are. If you believe that you have the ability and the authority to change your behavior, then you have and you will.

Don't forget that when I say you can change your nature, I do not mean that you discard the old you and become a new you. You also change your nature by increasing your choices to respond in new ways and create a series of new behaviors which you did not previously possess. NLP never removes choices, only increase them, but you may well find that you no longer choose to do the behaviors that you used to, because they are no longer important to you.

* * * * * * * *

There is another type of choice that we haven't looked at yet which is pretty relevant to today's world.

People have far more choices than they realise they have. I hear people complaining about the company they work for, yet they choose to work for it. They complain about the rail service they use, yet they choose to travel by rail. They complain about anything and everything, when what they are doing in their lives, and the problems they consider themselves to be suffering, are all as a result of a series of choices they have made, and are continuing to make, day after day.

Many people will say that they have no choice around these topics.

Here is a tough statement. There is always a choice.

If you are in a position to read that statement, you are in a position to make choices in your life. (If you are a 12 year old working in a slate quarry in India, you are probably not, but a child in that situation will not be reading this book). In your situation, there may not be a choice about what has happened to you in your life, but there is always a choice about what you think about what has happened to you. People are creating their lives. They do not have to be the victims to fate that they believe themselves to be.

There are of course things that happen over which you have no control. You may well once have been in, or maybe you are in right now, a situation not of your direct choosing. Sometimes it is as a consequence of your actions, and sometimes it is as a result of that well-known maxim 'shit happens'. More of this later, but the bottom line is that we are empowered to change the way we live our life.

Some time ago, Jenny, a friend of mine had a job that she was intellectually but not emotionally equipped to do. She suffered from stress as result. This made her ill and she had to take time off work. She would frequently complain about her work, and her stiff neck, and her nausea, and her anxieties, and that she had headaches – all the signs of stress. But never once did she speak of giving up her job, and taking another closer to her home that would be a better match for her emotional state and allow her to feel less stressed. Everyday, when she could, she would go to work and continue to live the lifestyle that was causing her so much unhappiness. She never realised she was making that decision. She never saw that she had a choice. After several years she was made redundant. She complained of course, how they didn't understand, how unfair it was after all the effort she had put in and how her work was her

The Self-Help Delusion

life. She didn't realise that it was the best thing that could have happened to her. Her health improved dramatically as a result, and she was much happier in herself. She met a lovely man, perhaps because she had more time to look for lovely men, got married and lived happily ever after – or not as the case may be, as we lost contact over twenty years ago.

People – in the western world anyway - choose to work where they work, travel how they travel, live how they live, sleep with who they sleep with and marry who they marry. We are not the victims that we often believe ourselves to be.

You may have a belief that you cannot choose where you work. There may be no jobs in your area that would pay enough to allow you to live the way you do. The obvious answer is to change how you live and where you live.

That of course would mean that you would have to sell your home, and re-locate, uproot the kids from school and cause major family and social upheaval. Well, I hear you say, I don't want to do that. So you have decided against doing that. Then you are choosing to continue to work where you do.

Seemingly nothing will change; yes it will. You have now realised that you have exercised a choice. You are choosing to work where you do, with all its inconveniences, in preference to moving to another locality. You just don't fancy any of the alternatives you have considered.

Sometimes another person comes along and helps you to be aware of alternatives that you hadn't considered. That is one reason why people need people to help them grow and develop, and this is where a mentor or coach can be useful to you.

So here is the significant point. You may well continue to do what you are doing already, but what you have changed is your perception of who is in charge of your life. You are at cause when you realise that your lifestyle is of your choosing. You cannot blame fate or your partner or your family or tradition or anything else. You are choosing to do what you do now because of unconscious decisions made perhaps years ago, and you have now decided consciously that you do not want to do anything else instead.

You are now aware in your conscious mind that you are 'making a decision'. When you realise that it is your decision, you are in a position to review it and to consciously decide if you want to continue to live your life in the same way, doing the same job, living in the same place etc. And that realisation is called empowerment.

It's not what we do, or what happens to us, that is so significant, it's what we think about what we do or what happens to us that matters. Most people don't realise that. It's those thoughts and your subsequent actions following on from those thoughts that create change in your life, not the things that happen to you.

When something 'bad' happens to you, your life will change and your life experiences will be different from then on. I agree that you would not have changed your life if your circumstances hadn't changed, but they have, and so 'no change' is now not an option. The only option you do have is 'what do I choose to think about this, and what do I choose to do in the light of the new situation.' It's your behavior now that changes your life.

A few years ago, I was made redundant at age fifty-seven from a company where I had worked for thirteen years. In many ways, I think I unconsciously engineered my own redundancy, but that's a long story. I was not particularly surprised, and it took me only a few days to accept it and to feel at ease with my new situation. But the people I worked with had a much harder time accepting it. 'If they make you redundant, what hope is there for me?' was a common comment. Several others made redundant at the same time expressed a 'why me, what have I done to deserve this, this is unfair' approach to their 'fate'. I recognised it as an opportunity to change my lifestyle, and begin again in a new direction. Without it, I doubt if I would have had either the courage or the money to create a new life. I am eternally grateful both to the man who enforced the change, and to my beliefs that made my new life possible.

Many people have a serious problem with enforced changes in their lives but, armed with these beliefs, I did not.

I know that some people will sit and spend the rest of their lives, or at least the next few years complaining that life has treated them unfairly, and whilst that may well be true, not to be treated unfairly was not an option they had. The point is; what do they do now.

The man who decided to make me redundant was my greatest asset. A useful belief is that other people are your greatest asset, and the reverse is also true, that you are another person's greatest asset.

There's a beautiful quote from Neale Donald Walsh 'Other people see their possibilities in the reality of you'.

It's easier sometimes for you to see routes that another might use to achieve what it is they say they want, but, for one reason or another, they hadn't recognised as a possibility. I went to Grammar school, and left at sixteen with no qualifications. The idea of working at school to go to university was never in my head, nor was it in the heads of my parents either. There was nobody in my life to put that idea there. To use a modern concept, it wasn't even grayed out on my menu of options. Indeed, it wasn't even on my menu of options.

My children went to university because it was the first item on their menu of things to do after school. Neither my wife nor I ever said, 'you will go to university.' or in any way suggested that they 'should'. For them it was just a natural progression in the process of their education.

A choice is a choice only if we realise it's a choice, and it's our job to point out opportunities to others to assist them to achieve their objectives; in the nicest possible way of course. See 'Advisements' in a later chapter)

To sum up, reactions come from the unconscious mind, instinctive and driven by history whereas responses come from the conscious mind after the application of a little rational thought.

You are not a victim if you realise that 'it's not what happens to you in this life, it's what you **think** about what happens to you' that determines the choices that are available to you whilst you are creating your life.

The Process of Changing

> *The greatest revolution of our generation is the discovery that human beings, by changing the inner attitudes of their minds, can change the outer aspects of their lives.*
> William James

We all change as we move through life. Everything is always changing.

To quote the song writer Jewel 'Everything is temporary if you give it enough time'.

As each day dawns, you are changed from yesterday. Physical changes are obvious when we are young. Later, we know that our body is changing, but the change is not so easy to measure or even to notice over a short period of time. But as the months and years go by, the changes in ourselves and our world become more noticeable. As we live our day to day lives, most people do not often think abut how they have changed, they just take each day as it comes.

Try and remember yourself as you were once, when you were at school, first Junior and then Senior; the simple naive innocent going out on your first date, and your first part time job. You will no doubt remember various events from those years, but it's doubtful if you can remember the way you saw the world then, or remember the you that you were then. You can no doubt create pictures in your memory of yourself and the world you inhabited then, but that's not the you or the world as then, it's the you and the world you are now looking back on.

The only record you might have of the physical you of that time would be a measurement on the kitchen wall with your increasing height marked every Christmas or birthday or New Year, together with a few school reports which your parents saved with pride or perhaps despair, and perhaps photos of the physical you as then. That is not the part of you that matters, not the internal you. Of that you, you have little or no memory. What you may have tucked away in your memory is the story that you have been telling yourself and others since, whenever you reminisce of those times, about the you that you were then.

Change has taken place in you since then, and will continue to take place in you for the rest of your life, until that ultimate permanent change that is our inevitable eternity.

Your life may well not have panned out for you in quite the way you thought it might. Parts have of course, but overall, perhaps not.

When I say, 'panned out for you' I'm not talking about your social success, or your material security, the number of cars you own or the value of your house, or even your standing in society. I'm talking of that part inside; the you that is you that only you know about, that part of you that only you inhabit?.

Bottom line is, are you happy with all of yourself and the way you are now?

You've probably taken on new beliefs, or changed some old ones over the last say 10 years, but did you consciously realise that change was happening, and that you would inevitably be different in say ten years time? I don't think many people do. We are quite prepared to change the outer trappings of our life, but we usually do nothing about our personal internal selves.

The question you perhaps might like to ask yourself is 'Do I now want to consciously direct the manner of my changing, or leave it to the external forces of my life?'

So far, I'm suggesting that you have left it up to life to happen to you.

And maybe now you would like to start consciously creating your life?

That's really why I wanted to write this book. Because I meet more and more people who are seriously questioning the objectives of their life. Maybe they have more time now. The working week

The Self-Help Delusion

has reduced over the last 50 years, and there is more thinking time available to many. When people were down the mine or in a factory for 12 hours a day, 6 days a week, and church twice on Sundays, there wasn't much time to ponder the trials of life; you accepted the beliefs you were given, and just got on with it.

Now that there is time to think, more and more people are expressing a feeling of incompleteness, and searching round outside of themselves for something to complete them.

And it doesn't have to be that way. To achieve physical goals, you may exercise daily because you believe that if you do, you will feel better for it, and tomorrow you will be closer to the 'ideal' you. It takes a lot of effort to change the way your body is growing, both by changing what you eat, and in the way you use your body in your efforts to achieve your desired goals. But experience tells us, and our fitness guru at the local gym tells us, exactly what to do and how to do it. And when we persist, there is no doubt that the results will begin to manifest themselves.

In this book, I am suggesting ways to achieve peace of mind goals. If you feed your body rubbish food, you will not be the healthiest or the fittest that you can be. In the long term, if we consume nicotine and tar, sulfur and other carcinogens, we will have to pay the price with a shorter life or experience poor health, or if we are really unfortunate, both. It does take some time and effort, and the physical results are of course very easy to measure.

In a similar way, we need to examine the 'food' with which we continually feed our conscious mind and which the unconscious mind uses to create our future. The question is, what mental food can we 'consume' so that the mind can practice creating our desired future, and be in a position to produce the results we want for our future contentedness.

I am likening your psychological 'body' to your physical body That you should be mindful of what you think, what you say, what you see, and what you read, the stuff you are feeding your mind, in the same way that you might watch what you eat and drink and how you exercise.

This seems tough, but everything you experience, think, say, see and read is stored away in your unconscious mind to influence your thoughts and actions later. An awareness of even just this will help you to look again at the events of your life.

I was on holiday in Switzerland some years ago. I was on my own, and totally chilled out. Life as a tourist there is wonderful, and I made good use of the extensive transport system. I don't speak much French or German and so for two weeks I had no negative stuff coming into my mind. No winging and complaining, no newspapers, no television; only the joy of being there with the lakes and mountains and forests. Then I came back to England and on my first day back to work, on the train, the person opposite had a newspaper with the headline 'Another teenager raped and murdered'.

And then I knew what I had been missing.

I don't believe any social good is served by pages and pages of detail after detail of rapes, murders, social injustices and stories about socially inadequate people. The Victorians used to go to the lunatic asylum and pay a penny to watch the dysfunctional inmates. We still do that; it's called 'Big Brother'.

The public need to know what has happened, but when the details are intended only to sell more papers by creating as much shock - horror as possible, I do not believe that is useful to the minds of the people who read it. It creates a fear out of all proportion to the dangers, and it creates knee jerk reactions which often result in unjust laws, or vigilantes.

Unfortunately, most people don't see it like that because they have been conditioned by the society we live in to think of it as normal. For them it is, and I find that sad.

I had direct experience of this behavior pattern a year or two back. Our parents have both died, and my sister and I were the last of my family. She lived alone, and I visited when I could. I had a problem with this in that, though I loved my sister, in order to maintain a positive relationship with her, I had to mirror and match her negative complaining attitude to the world. Over several years, I found myself becoming a grumpy old man, finding fault in everything. Fortunately I was conscious of this and did my best to protect myself by following her conversation three steps behind as it were, and never leading it. But I couldn't be me with her, as we

The Self-Help Delusion

would just argue whenever I tried. My dear sister died in 2009 with total organ failure, mainly as a result of smoking 20 a day for 40 years. And there was nothing I could do about that either.

People will do as people do, and change can only come from them, no matter how much you would like them to do differently.

To direct psychological change requires the same sort of persistence and focus as for physical change. Psychological change is often considered the more difficult task, indeed many people considerer it impossible, and say things like 'I am what I am, take me, or leave me', and of course, with that belief, they are correct. For them, it is impossible. Henry Ford said: "Whether you believe you can, or you believe you can't, you will be right".

There is another saying by that well known author Anon: "If you always do what you've always done, you'll always get what you've always gotten."

You have to do something different. Studying books on physical fitness does not make you fit. Joining a gym does not make you fit. Going to a gym does not make you fit. You have to do the exercises to make you fit. That's what makes the difference and creates changes.

I've meet many people who want things to be different in their lives, but they don't want to change anything about themselves. They are OK, it's the world and other people that are wrong and they set out with stoic determination to change the world so that they can live more happily in it. And they do it for years, sometimes for all their life and they never realise that this approach does not work.

The world and other people will not change just because you want them to. It's not the world's job to make you happy.

The only strategy that will enable you to live in contentedness is when you change the only thing you have control over – your behavior.

And that's often a hard fact to digest.

Behavior, at least in my definition, consists of three parts. Thought, Word, and Deed. What you believe and think, what you say to yourself and others, and what you do in your life.

We will discus many thoughts throughout this book, but no

matter how firmly you espouse them, only when followed by a change in deed will external events change in your life. Do not fall into the trap of thinking that the thoughts and words will of themselves create change. I know several people who are experts in their problem, but they still have their problem.

To change what you do, first you need to change your beliefs, which of course includes what you think, expect, fantasise, imagine. Then you need to change the words you use to express those thoughts to yourself and to others, and then you will find it will be far easier to change your actions.

This is not a trivial process. It's a total review of every aspect of the way you live your life.

Remember, up to now in your life you have been making it up as you went along, allowing life to push and pull you, buffet and swamp you and you have been re-acting and creating all sorts of ill considered beliefs, and half formed values. I'm offering you an alternative approach to your life, where you create your life with conscious thought, with volition.

Before the scientific era, things just happened. There was no thought that there could be or indeed had to be any other cause but God. God was very active in those days, well, he was a young God I suppose, and had all this energy to spare. He was given the credit and the blame for lots of things that happened in the world. Acts of God were very common.

In this highly scientific world, we have the concept of cause and effect. That is to say, an event happens because something causes it to happen. There can be no effect without a cause to create it. In the western world, at least among the atheists and agnostics, God is not considered as a cause.

So here's key question for you. Are you 'at cause' in your life, or 'at effect'? By asking yourself the question, you are becoming aware that perhaps much of your behavior is a re-action to external forces, rather than a response to the here and now events of life that just happen to you.

It's easy to think that you are at cause in your life as you obviously cause the little things to happen, where you go to shop for your groceries and things like that, but you may not be so sure about the events in the bigger picture.

If you believe that you are an innocent bystander in your life, and that the best you can do is to sit back, and when an event happens to you, re-act to it, then the power to effect change in your life lies outside you. You would have no power to change anything and deep down, you will see yourself as a victim, like a boat on a rough sea, just riding out the rough times, with no rudder, and no power to steer to a port.

If you realise that you really are creating the world that you are living in, through your responses to the stimuli to your nervous system and your stored remembrances and that your expectations of the future and your behavior in the world is as a result of your own creation, then you are at cause in your life. You are making it happen, and you know you are making it happen, and the power to effect change in your life lies inside you.

If we are creating our reality in our heads, as you may well believe after reading this book even if you don't already, which of these beliefs will be most useful to take on board and act as though they were true?

Most people don't see it like that, in such cut and dried terms. Most people believe there are some things at which they are at cause, but for some things they are at effect. When they get a head cold, they believe they are at effect, that they didn't cause it, and to believe otherwise is crazy. Maybe it is, but the body carries all the time many common viruses that cause illnesses, but generally we don't get ill. The question is not 'why do you get sick?' The question is 'why do you get sick now?'

A friend of mine has an eating disorder. We were chatting about it on one occasion, and I asked the question. 'When did you decide to create this problem?' She stopped dead in her tracks. After a moment she told me when and why she created it. Nobody had ever asked her that before. And of course, if you believe that you created it, you can believe that you can un-create it. I'm pleased to say that she is well on her way to un-create her problem, and shortly she won't do the problem any more.

What Are You?

Before you begin to look at changing your life, perhaps you need to ask yourself what or who are you now? What constitutes you, the you inside that talks to you; that feels good or bad, happy or sad, weak or strong? That question has been asked by man, of man, since man could think, and philosophy began. How do you define yourself to yourself? Who or what do you think you are?

In answering the question, it's easy to provide a resume, a CV. Those are the facts. They describe your physical existence and you could go on to describe the roles you play or have played in this life. You could give me your CV and we could talk for hours. But that is all. They do not describe you, that part of yourself I call 'the you that is you'. So again I ask you, what or who are you?

I think that first, you are a sentient being. That is, you are aware of yourself. Aware that you are asking yourself, 'Who am I' and also aware that the answer is not obvious.

It's easy to think that you are your body. Obviously you are. You wouldn't be here without your body but let's look at the inverse. Is your body you?

I think it's evident that it's not the total you. It's the part of you that takes up space in the world, but that's obviously not the total of you. I'm suggesting that it is not a useful idea to think that you are your body. You own your body. You may be very proud of the way it looks. You may have worked on it, and as a result you have a body that perhaps better serves you in your ambitions and your daily life.

I am personally aware that as I become older, my body is less attractive to some people than it used to be, and it's true that I am not as fit as I used to be, and I don't get the same enjoyment from physical exercise that I used to, but generally it only limits my physical options, not my options to be what I want to be as a human being.

We cannot really think of ourselves without a body, as it's an intrinsic part of who we are in this life. But I am suggesting that you are more than that. Your body isn't you. Think instead, that your body is only a packing case. Without it on this earth, you would not be here. Well, you might, but not in the usual sense. Your body serves a purpose only in this earthly existence.

So am I saying that you are more than your body? Not even that. I'm saying that there is no part of you that is your body. You own your body at this point in your existence, but it has nothing to do with you. Most people believe that their body is part of them, or perhaps, that they are part of their body, but look at it this way. You drive a car – yes? Are you your car; is any part of you your car? No, of course not. If your car gets old and develops rust spots, you are not in anyway less than you were before. If your car breaks down and you cannot move around in it as you used to, you are still not less than you were?

So it is with your body. Or at least, it is useful way to think of your body in the same way. Look at your hand. Is that you? Every cell in your body (except perhaps your brain and your spinal cord) is being replaced at different rates. Bones may take several years, skin cells are being replaced every few days. If you spill indelible ink on your fingers – as I did by accident recently – within 3 days it had worn off. That's because the skin that was stained is replaced by un-stained skin, and the marks disappear. The hand you are looking at now is not the hand you were looking at 3 days ago. If you had that hand amputated, would you be any different from now, other than that you only have one hand, and you might have to make different decisions as to how you would make your way in the world - as when your car is in the garage being serviced. Your body would be short of a hand; your life short of a car. But would the you that is you be the lesser without it?

It's not the loss of the hand that would change you, it's what you make it mean in your life that will create the change in your world.

Your body and its appearance do of course affect what happens

The Self-Help Delusion

to you, say, in the way another person responds or reacts to you. That aspect of you, your appearance, is part of the cause of the way people react to you. Much of the rest of their reaction to you is the other messages that you are sending them.

The point here is, are you your body? And my answer is no. You are not your body. I realise that you are perhaps not fully accepting of that way of thinking yet but you are now aware of the thought.

The next question you might ask yourself is, are you your mind? Your instinctive answer to that is no doubt 'Yes, of course' and most people would never think to question it. Your mind seems to have something to do with what or who you think we are. But which part of your mind: the thinking mind, the logical mind, the creative mind, the frightened mind, the rational mind. And here's a thought. If you are your mind, what part of you steps back as it were and observes the passage of emotions through your mind and listens to the dialog that is an almost continuous part of your consciousness? Not monolog notice, but dialog. The anger, the laughter, the suddenly awareness of yourself when you are speaking to another - especially when in front of many others, when you hear your own voice, and suddenly realise that it is you talking. Which part of you is doing the realising?

Some philosophies call that part 'The observer', because it seems to be a separate part of ourselves, watching what the other parts are doing.

So perhaps it's your observer that is the real you. If that were true that would then mean that the parts of the mind and the emotions that it observes are not you. Part of your mind is creating your emotions. At one moment they rise to prominence, and some time later, if you are fortunate, they fall away and disappear. You are no more the thoughts that pass through your mind, than the sky is the clouds that pass across it.

None of these ideas are new. They have all been floating around for some time; some for thousands of years. People have been here before, trying to make sense of it all. The difference is, they were looking for the truth; I'm just looking for what is useful to us whilst working our way through life.

I'm asking you questions so that you can find your own answers.

They will be your truth – at this moment. Do not forget though, that we are all works in progress, and your truth now may not be your truth later. In some ways, I hope it isn't, or you are going to gain nothing from reading this book. When you answer questions, you have to ask yourself what is true for you, not, what have I learned of what is, or was, true for another. Somewhere between the input from outside yourself, and the input from inside yourself, you will create your own truth.

Ultimately, we are making it all up and we have the power, when we realise it, to make it up in a different and more useful way.

The next question is, do you think you are your behavior? Most people do. And I've come to believe that that is not a useful belief to have either. It seems to me that a person's behavior is their activity in response or reaction to their interpretation of the stimulus that their brain received.

The process seems to be:

You receive stimulus from your senses. This stimulus may be incomplete or distorted somehow, dependent upon the event causing it. For example, you may miss-hear something because the stimulus did not impact your ear with enough energy to cause a complete message to your brain. This is one reason why older people can seem stupid because they only hear half of a conversation, and guess the rest to try and make sense of it; to give some intelligent response. This is known as confabulation.

You interpret that stimulus – in the only way you can, through deletion, distortion, and generalisation of that stimulus.

You create a meaning – dependant upon your history and the state of mind you are in at the time. You react or respond in a certain way – the only way you know how given your conscious and unconscious objectives.

Note that I have two very distinct meanings for reaction and response.

A response is created in the conscious mind, with consideration of the here and now. A reaction is created from our history by the unconscious mind.

A re-action is acting as we did before, for the same reasons when we first received the stimulus. At that time, it was a response and may well have been appropriate. Now it is a re-action and not necessarily appropriate in the here and now. In fact, almost always, simply by its definition, it will not be the best – most useful – of behaviors.

So, following this argument, your behavior is your response to the stimulus received, either from outside your head in the now, or from inside your head as a result of the meaning that you created for the stimulus when you first received it some time in your history. From this we can conclude that you are more than your behavior, and indeed, your behavior is not you. The English language causes us to conclude that you are your behavior, with expressions such as "I am angry" as though I = anger and I am my behavior of anger. And when we use these expressions, we consolidate the erroneous belief that we are our emotions. These thoughts may seem trivial, inconsequential, and pedantic. They are, but they are not. Be careful what you say, for that is the way you will create your world.

This is not a new-age get-out for not being responsible for anything. "It wasn't me wot done it your honor, it was just my response to the situation, and nothing to do with me" or words to that effect. Many people who are steeped in the old way of thinking interpret it that way, but that is not what I am saying. I said that you are not your behavior. I did not say that you are not responsible for it. At some level, you chose to do whatever you do. You cannot then say that you had nothing to do with it.

We play many roles in life as we interact and live / work with other people. Sometimes perhaps we would like to play a different role in a particular person's life, but they don't want to play the other role, and it takes two to tango.

When on a professional development training course, we may be asked to pretend to be a manager, or a customer or a salesperson or a help-line operative etc.

In the environment of the training course, we take on the role of one person to learn and practice how to interact with another person who is also playing a role. But I don't think for a moment that we believe we are the character that we are pretending to be.

We play the part and act the role to enlarge our understanding and experience of that part of the work environment.

We play roles in our life too of course. We learn to play more and more roles as we get older. Dependent on where you are in your life, you will have played some of the roles of child / pre-teen / teenager / lover / partner / husband / wife / father / mother / grandfather / grandmother etc.

Then of course there are the roles we play at work, In my working life I have played the roles of: garage mechanic, teacher, shop keeper, software developer, salesman, support analyst, CEO of my own company, account manager, personal trainer, personal help line consultant, writer and a whole lot of things in between.

And I played those roles to the full. I performed each for somewhere between four and seven years, and in that time I took on the beliefs and thoughts and actions and attitudes necessary to play those roles, and I played so seriously that I couldn't tell where the role ended and I began. After a few years in each role, I got bored because as each Christmas came and went, I realised that I was no further forward in my own personal growth than I had been the previous Christmas. I had to change my role - to begin again - and to learn to play a new role. And in some magical, mysterious, heaven-sent way, the opportunities to change roles came my way.

But here's the point, I have remained me throughout all of these roles, but I am a very different me to the one I was when I was a naive sixteen year old educationally failed apprentice garage mechanic. I know more now, I understand more, I am perhaps a little wiser that I was. The 'me that is me' was never any of the roles; I just thought I ought to be at the time.

Looking back on those times, I have always felt an outsider. Always felt that I was playing at the part I'd assigned myself at that time in my life. That made it easier for me to take on board the belief that 'I am not my behavior'. I realise now that I was playing the role as I created the need for that role in my life.

At some point, I may well have to learn to play the part of a grumpy old man in a retirement home.

I've been very fortunate in that all my life I've really only done things that interested me. Though I didn't realise it at the time, I've changed a hobby or an interest in my private life, and created the opportunity to make my living doing it. I say that I 'created the opportunity'.

The question I ask myself to determine my truth is 'was it good fortune; was it just luck, or chance or fate or what?' I'll cover luck and chance and fate later.

Some believe that I sent a message out to the universe that I was an opportunity waiting to happen to it, and the universe brought that opportunity into my life. I know that sounds very fanciful, and there is no way it can in anyway be proved. But when an opportunity came my way, I recognised it as such, and generally I grabbed it with both hands, and never regretted a single thing.

That explanation doesn't work for me.

Back in earlier chapters we spoke about the unconscious mind deleting most of the data coming in from our senses, and only passing to the conscious mind, that which the conscious mind has expressed an interest in. Once that interest has been expressed, the unconscious mind will allow through, details that might help the conscious mind achieve the expressed desires. After all, would you notice a shop on the high street selling baby clothes if you have no baby in your life? When you purchase a particular type of car, you notice everybody is driving them. We only notice what we are looking for.

Having said that about the universe, the only interview I've had for a job was when I was 23, and applied for my first lecturing role. After that, as a result of what is now called networking, I was simply offered roles I wanted. It's a fact that the majority of roles / jobs in business and industry are filled as a result of networking. I just called it friendship with all I came into contact with, never with any ulterior motive.

Sometimes we have made a decision that did not produce the results we sought. I don't believe in mistakes. I think it's just as important to find out what you don't want, as much as to find what you do. Each of our behaviors may or may not lead to what we had in mind when we thought it or said it or did it. All that our behaviors do is to bring opportunities into our life, and we can then ask ourselves the question, now what? What do I think or say or do in the light of the here and now. If the results are what I wanted, I carried on with the plan. If not, I did something different until what I wanted did come into my life. Or I changed my preferences, and moved in a different direction, and learned to play a different role.

Sometimes I think that I have led a charmed life. Sometimes, I think that a charmed life has led me. I know that some people have so many 'bad' things happen to them, and sometimes, after that, they manage to make things even worse for themselves by making perhaps unenlightened decisions about what to do next. Some people make enlightened decisions, and still 'bad' things happen.

An oft asked question is 'why do bad things happen to good people'.

My answer to that is, 'Why would you expect anything else?' Often things don't actually happen to you, they just happen to the person who happens to be in that position, in that space, at that time. The happening has nothing to do with you. You just happen to be there.

Sometimes things happen to you as a result of your previous behavior. Sometimes we do things we regret, and when we do, there is often a price to be paid. That can be there and then, or it may be several years later.

In this life, sometimes the price is set by another's relationship with you, and other times it affects your relationship with yourself.

Bad things happen to good people because of the old adage, 'Shit happens'. To quote; 'the rain falls on the just and the unjust alike'. Leading a good life is about your behavior. You are not rewarded for this, either in this life or the next. It's just what you do. If the knife artist is walking down the same ally way as you, through no fault of your own, you can be hurt. Shit happens.

We cannot send conscious messages to the universe. It has no ears to hear our sobbing, no eyes to see our tears, no nose to smell our fear, no heart to feel our happiness. The messages we send come from that part of us over which we have no conscious control, from our unconscious mind; our soul if you like. And we do not know what those messages contain except that they will reflect what we think we want for ourselves, rather than what we will for ourselves.

The Self-Help Delusion

Some time earlier, I said that some people believe that we create our illnesses, our own pain; our own discomforts. However, the plagues that wiped out half of Europe in the Middle Ages were not brought about by the unconscious mind, or the collective consciousness of the better part of half the population. And it wasn't God either, though most people at the time believed it was.

I've only recently realised that when I communicate I have a habit of trying to get past the roles set by the situation and get to the real person behind the role. Some people are happy to be people, and others not. Even after weeks or months of contact, a person will steadfastly refuse to be a person rather than the role they are playing.

Roles held by people promoted beyond their confidence, and maybe their ability are the most difficult to break down. Generally known as jobsworths, they dare not be themselves. They feel that they need to shelter behind the role they have been given because to step outside their role would put them outside their comfort zone. In Victorian times, role was everything. The master and his lady could talk of their most intimate doings, even in the presence of servants because servants were considered as almost sub human, and so did not count. On the other hand, servants did not like familiarity from their lords and masters for exactly the same reasons; the idea that all people are equal even if not the same is a late 20th century phenomenon.

The key thing is to realise that in almost every moment of our lives, we are playing a role. Sometimes the role involves another; sometimes just ourselves.

We have all created a role for ourselves. It's called personality. Young people are more flexible in behavior than older people – generally – because they haven't yet created their role in life and they try on various behaviors just to see if they fit the personality they want to represent them.

Just sometimes we meet someone with whom we feel that we don't have to play a role, and we can just be the 'me' role. I think the greatest compliment you can pay anyone is summed up in the statement. "When I'm with you, I can be me".

So I'm suggesting that you not consider yourself as your body, your mind or your behavior. This leaves the begging question, what are you?

For me, I am really my higher self. The observer, as eastern philosophies would have it, your soul if you are into souls as many religions would have it.

Don't forget. I'm not telling you the truth. The ideas presented above provide for an alternative way to see the world, and they may be more useful that those you have had up to now.

The Creation of Meaning

"Men are not disturbed by things, but the view they take of things." - Epictetus (55-135 A.D.)

I want for us to look at meaning. What do actions and events mean, and where does that meaning come from? Most people have a belief that the meaning of an event is part and parcel of that event.

I'll start with an NLP quotation "Nothing has meaning but the meaning you give it" And I think the writer did indeed mean 'nothing' has meaning including, presumably, this quotation.

Shakespeare said, "Nothing is right or wrong, but thinking makes it so.' which broadly amounts to the same thing.

There are some questions that follow naturally from the two quotations.

'What is the meaning of life? - Does life have a meaning outside of the person living it? Is there a universal meaning, irrespective of whether we find it or not?

In short, why are we here? What is the meaning of life?

These are big questions.

As I see it, it's like this. The very question, 'What is the meaning of life?' has a pre-supposition in it. The danger of a question with a pre-supposition is that any answer you give accepts the pre-supposition. As in the classic 'Have you stopped beating your wife yet?' An answer of 'Yes' or 'No' still leaves you with a beaten wife.

The presupposition in the question 'What is the meaning of life?' is that life has a meaning. A cleaner question might be: 'Does life have a meaning, and if so, what is that meaning?'

Some people spend their entire lives looking for 'The meaning of life', (including Monty Python.) attempting to locate or discover why we are here. Some simply accept that we are, and enjoy it. One thing for sure; most people think that there is a meaning in events that they need to understand, the meaning, the one meaning.

Most people think – believe - that meaning is the inherent property of an event, rather than being the property of the person who has created it in their head.

In this chapter I will show that this belief is mistaken, in that there are several ways to 'see' things, or to attribute meaning, and they are all valid.

Most people, at one time or another use the expression 'Everything happens for a reason', and I'm not going to tell you that it doesn't. Everything does happen for a reason. But here's the colossal shift in your belief; you create the reason.

The reason - or meaning – of the event is created during or after the event, by you, not before the event by some outside entity. To think otherwise would mean that God, fate, luck, chance, destiny or whatever had predetermined the meaning, and then created the event to see if you can work out what it really means.

It's not useful to have a belief that life is a game of trying to work out what has already been planned for you. At least, I don't think it is. Life is about your planning your life for yourself. Life is not a massive guessing game, where we run around desperately trying to understand the pre-determined meaning in events - unless of course you want it to be.

You have the power to decide for yourself what the events in your life mean. You see, in the end, meaning, like belief, has to be made up. Religions of course have the truth about this, a big banner in the sky that provides a meaning from on high, directly written by the deity.

Sorry, all meanings have been made up – created, if you prefer – by somebody at sometime even if it was 2000 years ago. What we tend to do is to take someone else's meaning and assume, because, in some cases, it's a popular and long established meaning, that it must be the true meaning.

When my son was at university studying philosophy, we talked

The Self-Help Delusion

sometimes, and in response to what I said, would reply with 'Kant said that', or Aristotle, or Hegel or whoever, and what they said they thought were the truth. I told him that I'm not really interested in what those great philosophers thought. Now, as he knows that I am usually an inquisitive man, he didn't understand until I told him, that I'm not really interested in what these people thought was the truth, I'm only interested in what I think is the truth. The ancient philosophers spoke some universal truths, but they also promulgated ethical and scientific nonsense.

I've been told that I am a 'Post Modernist'. I have to arrive at my own truth and my own meaning for life, love and the pursuit of happiness. On the other hand, in order to do that, I think you have to expose yourself to what others think, and then see if it matches with your truths, and then take those ideas on board as yours if it does.

Some people across the racial, intellectual and financial spectrum spend their entire lives trying to find, discover, uncover and search for the meaning in everything that happens to them, and never realise that there is no meaning in anything - to discover or anything else - only a meaning that we each create and espouse as our own.

It's really all a question of what does 'it' mean to you and what can you make 'it' mean to you. The 'it' of course is anything and everything. Your parent's divorce, the colour of your toilet paper, the conjunction of the planets when you were born, why certain things seem to happen to you, why bad things happen to good people, why good things happen to bad people, why things seem to happen in threes, life, death, the star sign you were born under if you are into astrology, the numerical value of your name if you are into numerology and anything else you care to think of. Everyone is looking for the meaning in the event, as though the event had a meaning attached to it. And I don't believe it does. The meaning is not in the event. As with everything else, the meaning is in you.

Once we attribute responsibility for the events in our lives to luck or chance or fate, something outside of ourselves, we can easily see ourselves as victims in a cosmic game.

And that is not a useful belief because you have given away the power to create events (meaning) in your life to something outside of yourself. I believe it to be far more empowering to believe that you are the creator of all that events mean to you. Because if you believe that, then indeed you are the creator of all that happens to you. As you believe, so shall you make it. Don't forget, we are making it all up anyway. If you believe that you - and I mean the complete four parts of you we discussed earlier - if you believe that you are creating your life, the power for creating change lies inside you not outside you.

You see, mankind has always fought shy of taking responsibility for the things that happen to him. When we couldn't see any reason for the 'bad' things that happen we blamed God, an act of God. We did give him/her credit for the good things though, and in our prayers we give thanks for the good things. After all, if He caused the 'good' things to happen, it is only logical that He caused the 'bad' things to happen. That belief then led to them having to placate God, as clearly, man must have done something wrong.

In some earlier societies, by murder, we sacrificed human lives to please the God that society believed in.

In some current societies we sacrifice the living to please the God the leaders of those societies believe in, forcing people – generally women - to live lives of submission and subjugation.

Belief is the most powerful force on earth.

Some people still place the causes and the reasons for the apparent random events they experience to an outside intelligence.

There are some events we as individuals don't create – death and injury to those we love - and mankind as a collective force don't create: earthquakes, volcanoes, tornadoes, hurricanes. They are a natural consequence of the changes in the earth's structure, but outside of them, we, collectively and individually, we have created everything else. And we continue to create it, day by day, year by year. There is nothing in the future that is bound to happen other than the natural consequences of previous actions – credit crunch for one, global warming for another. We are making it happen. The stock markets don't move up or down according to some outside force from another planet. We, mankind; buyers, sellers, dealers, media predictors, a host of other people, we make it go up or

The Self-Help Delusion

down, following that well known rule, the self fulfilling prophesy. If enough influential people in the world believe that, say, a war with another country is inevitable, then that war will happen.

In 2001, George Bush had every intention of going to war with Iraq. All he was looking for was a meaning which he could sell to his government and the rest of the world. The meaning he sold was WMD, although it was obvious that most of us were not buying, it suited his politics and that of other hawks. Prime Minister Blair bought that reason and 'sexed up' reports to convince doubters that Britain could be attacked in 45 minutes. All nonsense of course, as Iraq had nothing to fire at us, and nothing to fire it with. The war became inevitable, and there was nothing the rest of the world could do to stop it.

Since then of course, we have been suckered into another war – Afghanistan and we have no chance of winning that one either, given any positive meaning for the word 'win'.

Belief is the most powerful force on earth.

We create our future, collectively, and individually, just as certainly as we created our past. We don't look back to history and say that event or that circumstance was not of man's making. Of course it was. Children working down the coal mines and of both genders sent out to be prostitutes as soon as they were physically big enough. All the injustice in the world and of course all the justice too, we created it all.

I wandered round Canterbury Cathedral the other day. It is full of the memorials to Colonel this and General that, commemorated for fighting in a foreign land, slaughtering the population who were fighting for their homeland, all for the meaning and the greater good and the egos of the British Government and Prime Minister. The memorials were in a church for God's sake. If society feels the need to commemorate these brave men, and they were brave men, that's fine, but for the church to collaborate and acquiesce to such injustice seems very odd to me.

You may be thinking, where is the relevance to me in all that? When I say we create our world, I don't mean that you physically create it. Unless you do. I made several items of furniture in my house. They would not be here had I not been here. But you didn't create Tower Bridge in London. You didn't create the Empire State Building in New York or the channel tunnel between England and France, someone else did. What you do create is the significance to you, the meaning of each event, emotion, experience, truth that presents itself in your life.

Take for example, the channel tunnel. It takes me on a train under the channel from the UK to the Continent.

That's the event. The consequence of course is that I arrive in France. The meaning, I create. To me, traveling through the tunnel is an emotional as well as a physical experience. There I am, sitting in a beautiful train, traveling at one hundred mph under the English Channel. People have dreamed of a channel tunnel for a hundred and fifty years. The Victorians even started to dig it until they ran out of money and realised that it was a step too far, creating it in their mind, imagining what it would be like if...

And now I am privileged to travel through that dream. Isn't that fantastic? With my iPhone and Bluetooth headphones, which are miracles in their own right, I listen to Bach's double violin concerto written over two hundred years ago. About half way through the tunnel, I walk along the corridor to the buffet car, and have a coffee in celebration of the courage, the drive, the dogged persistence of man that he should have dreamed it and eventually made it happen. And I am overwhelmed by the truth of it all. That's what the tunnel means to me. Or more precisely, that's what I have made the tunnel mean to me. It doesn't just take me on a train under the channel from the UK to the Continent; it takes me through a dream.

We all have to make meaning out of everything in order to process it, think about it and make decisions about it.

A useful way to consider and make sense of this is to think of meaning as the last part of a trilogy of three significant parts:

Event, Consequence and Meaning.

The Self-Help Delusion

The Event
I define an event as something that happens. It may be physical - a burnt finger say, or a missed appointment. It may be verbal where someone says something to you; it may be visual, where you have seen something – a sunset, or the waves breaking on a golden beach or another person behaving in a way you wish they hadn't. It would be the same event to anyone else as it is to you.

I'll use a dramatic example.

Say you have just stepped out of a bank having just concluded an appointment with your bank manger. You witness a shooting across the street and a man is shot and the villain ran off with the brief case belonging to the man who was shot. That was an event, and you saw it happen.

The Consequence
I define 'consequence' as being something that happens as a result of the event. The consequence will be the same irrespective of the people involved or the circumstances surrounding the event. It is directly connected to, and caused by the event. All events have consequences, even if it is something small like the event of not remembering to put money in your pocket and the consequence of not being able to buy the evening paper. In the case above, where the man was shot, one consequence might be that the man dies. Just to complicate things, a consequence of one event is often another event in its own right.

Another example

The event - A jockey falls of his horse.
The consequence – The jockey breaks his arm

It doesn't matter what state of mind the jockey was in when he fell, anyone who fell the way he did would have broken his arm. Cause leading to Effect, Event leading to Consequence.

The third part of the trilogy is;

The Meaning
I define meaning as your response to that event and its consequences. The consequence is as a result of the event, the meaning is your response or re-action to the consequence.

   1   2   3

Event -> consequence -> meaning
    Event-> consequence -> meaning
        Event-> consequence -> meaning -> etc

We run our lives following this pattern. Since we are able to multi-task, numerous strands of the above sequence are passing through our lives at any one time.

The jockey, in order to process the event creates a meaning for the event and its consequences. He has his arm in plaster and cannot ride for a few weeks. What does he think about this? What meaning does he create?

Does he mope around feeling sorry for himself, that fate is against him? He only needed a few more wins this season to become champion jockey. He has every right to feel angry, emotional, cheated, victimised, fated, and all manner of things.

However, because he knows that he has a choice as to what meaning to create, he thinks "I'm injured; I cannot change that at the moment. I'm also an experienced rider. How can I spend the time that I cannot ride? I could write a book, my memoirs, I could approach local radio to be asked for my comments or actually present racing live on the radio, I could approach the BBC, ITV or SKY to get a wider coverage, be a celebrity on chat shows and quizzes. I'll need an agent to sort this for me". He could perhaps set the scene for another career when he is too old to ride. This could be the best thing that could have happened to him.

Champions bounce back from serious events, near death experience, major setbacks in a career, or marital breakdowns, or abusive parents or whatever.

The Self-Help Delusion

So it goes like this:

An event happens to you.
A consequence is thereby created.
You then create meanings in your own mind in order to process this consequence.

Most of us of course take on the meanings that other people have provided. As when I was made redundant, I created my own meanings, and refused to take on board the meanings provided by others.

'This world is a dangerous place, it's not safe to walk anywhere these days.' is a meaning that you might attach to the event outside the bank. And needless to say, you might be in shock, or stunned and disturbed. Some people might even be traumatised, and have difficulty sleeping for a few nights. That sort of thing doesn't happen in most people's experience. What to do, run, hide, or rush to the man's help as he is lying on the ground?

Generally these responses would be appropriate.

However

Let's take the meaning away. What you really saw was someone holding a stick like object and pointing it at another person. There was a puff of smoke and a loud bang, the second person fell to the ground and the first person ran away.

That's all.

That's what you actually saw, with your meaning removed. The rest was a story you made up in your head as a result of adding meaning to the events and even the consequences in order to process it in your conscious mind. Very difficult to simply say what you saw. That has no meaning. The human mind has a need to make up a story to make sense of what has been experienced.

What you didn't see was the film crew further along the road. In fact no one was hurt and five minutes later, the scene was re-enacted to make slight changes to the camera angle. The man who was killed was actually a woman in a man's suit, the gun wasn't a real one, and the puff of smoke did not come from an explosion.

If you had not been in the bank for over an hour, and you had seen the film crew setting up, the meaning you would have created in your mind would have been totally different. Of course, your state of mind as you left the bank also helped you to the meaning you created; that you had witnessed an act of robbery with violence.

So what you see with the meaning removed, what you actually see, is very different to the story you would tell if asked immediately after the event.

Experiments have been done in university, where a couple of people run into a class and wave guns and threaten the students. They then run out. Each student is asked to write down what they saw. Almost all accounts are different, because each student cannot keep from adding meaning to the event.

You could be asked as a witness to the event, and so much of what you would say, the way you would describe what you saw would have originated in your head, in the meaning you added to the event in order to make a story of it, rather than a factual report of what you actually saw.

The classic film 'Twelve angry men' is a perfect example of this, where 11 of the jury were prejudiced against the criminal because he was black, and created meanings from the evidence to 'prove' he was guilty.

Another film, called 'And the band played on' is a docu-drama about the rise of the AIDS virus and the people involved trying to understand and counter the spread of the disease. I thought it was brilliant, and poignant and moving and very well written. The team investigating the phenomenon that would later be called AIDS would meet every week and the first thing the leader wanted was answers to the three questions:

What do we think?

What do we know?

What can we prove?

They were brilliant questions to cut through the stories and

The Self-Help Delusion

'certainties' that the team members would inevitably add to the facts that had been uncovered during the preceding week,

Those three questions helped the team to face the reality that indeed there was often no new information to add to the picture they were building as to what the condition was, or how it was passed, even if it was passed from one person to another. It is so easy to add meaning to events without realising it. This meaning then becomes 'fact' in our mind, and we act on these 'facts' as though they were true.

In our lives, the above thoughts and realisations can help provide a more useful approach to many of the events and consequences that we experience. I realise that it is not as easy in practice as it is to read about, but becoming the observer and thinking of other meanings that would be more useful to you in that moment, seeing the process as events leading to consequences leading to the most useful meaning you can create for yourself.

A perhaps more relevant example:

You have decided that you like someone. You don't know them that well and you are not sure what they think of you, but it does matter that they think well of you. They said that they would 'phone you that evening to arrange to meet with you. The evening comes, and goes. No 'phone call. You are waiting in expectation for the call and it doesn't come. What do you think and what meanings do you create?

They changed their mind. They really don't want to see me; they just didn't have the courage to tell me at the time. In fact all people do that to me - say they'll see me and then decide not to. 'It must be me' you think, 'I'm just not attractive to the opposite sex. I'll never get married, nobody will love me. It's my lot in life'. . . .

Now of course you can say to yourself.

Q: 'What do I know? What do I actually know?'
A: 'I have not received a phone call.'

And that is all. Notice, not even 'They didn't ring' because you don't know that. There are many possible reasons why you did not receive a call.

They may have lost your number, or written it down incorrectly and 'phoned ten other people trying to find out your number.

They may have misheard your surname when looking it up in the book, and 'phoned the wrong number.

They may have stored your number on their mobile phone, and left it home when called away for the evening by their mother.

They may have transposed digits in your number and been dialing the wrong number.

There may have had a death in the family, and calling you is the last thing on their mind.

These are all possibilities. The only fact you know is that you have not received a phone call.

And you don't know why. So stop making up reasons, and beating yourself into submission with your fantasies.

Recently, I was asked to 'phone a client at his office on the following morning. My friend said, 'is that about a job'

I said 'I don't know.'

'Well, do you think he has a new contract for you'?

'I don't know.'

'Perhaps he will extend your existing contract'.

I don't know. At that point, I simply refused to waste my time speculating about the possible reasons for his wanting me to call him. I don't know. And I am happy with the not knowing. I will plan the day to give me time to perhaps go to see him and hear what he has to say, and listen to his proposals, but I refuse to spend time going through all the scenarios and my possible responses to them.

That's not easy to do, to just let it be, to be content with not knowing. It does become easier with practice when we realise that we unconsciously add our meanings to events, and it helps us to avoid this habit of adding the first meaning that comes to our head and then acting upon it as though it were the truth. We 'react', that is we re-act or act again, the way we did in the past. It's a habitual response to similar events that have happened in the past.

When the event is a disappointment, or an unpleasantness in our lives, sadly, that choice of habit is usually one that gives

The Self-Help Delusion

warmth, feels comfortable, allows me to blame someone else for my misfortune, hurt or pain.

It's strange, but there's a perverse comfort in giving that power of choice away to someone else. It then makes someone else responsible for your hurt, not you, and the resolution of that pain does not lie within your actions, but the actions of another. Someone else is responsible, but not you. You're just the innocent. You can then wallow in self-pity, feel sorry for yourself, feel self-righteous, indignant, misunderstood and badly treated by other people, and they should know better, and oh, if only other people would treat me the way I deserve, my life would be so much happier. But they don't, and you're not.

You have given away the responsibility for your happiness to someone else whose actions you cannot control.

These ideas can be really difficult to take on board, and if you take extreme cases they are more difficult to accept. So don't take extremes. Take simple cases in your life, and act as though all the foregoing is true.

How could someone add so much meaning to a simple event like a non existent 'phone call? But we all do it. And the more the event matters to us, the greater significance we give to the meanings we create.

* * * * * * *

I remember a while ago I went climbing in the Swiss Alps with Steve, a friend of mine with 25 years of mountain experience. We started in the valley, in the lush alpine meadow; climbed through the trees to the grassy alp above. Higher, past the short grass to the small stony outcrops, and then we went higher and higher, over the snow line, over the top of a glacier and then some climbing with hands and feet on the exposed rock. The terrain flattened out into a slow slope and a small peak at the summit. Eventually we reached the top. Well, he did; I wimped out with about 300 feet to go – an easy walk. I suffered serious angst. I had never been there before, never been that high before. London Bridge was my normal home ground. No real danger, no great risk. But I couldn't go on. It was all in my head. It wasn't the event; it was what I did with it in my head that created the reality (my reality) of danger and fear.

Another example. I was reared on war stories, and one I came across when I was about 12 years old was the story of Douglas Bader.

He had a flying accident before World War II. That was the event.

As a consequence, he had both of his legs amputated, one above the knee, and one below.

Most people would have spent the rest of their lives in a wheelchair, especially in 30's when prosthetic limbs and counseling was in its infancy. The meaning Bader created for that event and those consequences was that he would need new legs to be able to walk and fly an airplane. And that was about the only meaning he did create. He got his new legs, convinced the RAF that he could still fly, became a squadron leader, shot down enemy planes and was captured. He tried to escape twice, was captured again and was sent to Colditz Castle, the 'escape-proof' prison camp. After the war he worked the rest of his life in a normal business environment; with no legs.

Now I'm not suggesting for one moment that life is not different as a result of events that happen to you. Bader's certainly was, filled with pain and frequent opportunities for despair. But what events and consequences mean to you, in the short term and for the rest of your life, is always your creation - whether you realise it or not.

I said earlier that it's not what happens to us that create our lives, it's what we think about what happens to us.

I was made redundant, as I mentioned earlier. From that experience, the table opposite can be created:

You see my point? It's not the event that is important, it's what you think it means to you. Whatever you make it mean will be of your own creation. You can make it mean something constructive to you, or something destructive. The choice is always yours.

The Self-Help Delusion

Consequences	Do you make it mean this?	Or do you make it mean this?
I will lose the day to day social stimulus of the people I work with.	Life will be lonely. No one to talk to. All my life I've worked for that company and now they've just tossed me aside when it suited them.	I will make new friends who live nearer to my home, who more closely match my age and history, rather than those I've had to get along with at work.
I will have to spend my time in a different way	I just don't know what I will do with my time. I'll be bored stiff. Nothing to do all day.	I've now got time to do all those little things I never had time for before, and I can go back to the creative wood working that I used to love.
I will not receive an income from the company	How will I live? I'm broke. I won't starve, but I won't be able to afford to buy anything.	I can get a part time job nearer home, maybe even two. Less stressful, and far more healthy for me.
I will receive a lump sum of money	That won't last any length of time - the car will have to go.	I can invest that lump sum and add the interest to my part time money, and I can get a smaller car now, and go to evening classes to learning how to maintain it.

This is a very different way to think of the unpleasant events in your life. The events may be out of your control, but what you do about it afterwards is within your control, and that is what matters.

I don't know if it is true, but how much more empowering than thinking that the event itself has meaning.

* * * * * * *

I'm reminded of the horrific events that happened in England between July 1963 and October 1965 known as the 'moors murders'. Five children tortured and killed and the process recorded by one of the participants; a child screaming for its mother, another begging not to be burnt again. They were tortured and murdered and buried in unmarked graves, some of which (as I write this) have only recently been located, and the parents have now someplace to grieve. Other bodies are still somewhere out on the moor, in unmarked graves; a horrific story.

Nothing will ever compensate, nothing will ever provide recompense or justice or fairness. However, it's the parents for whom I feel the most sorrow; the parents, and their friends and relatives.

The suffering of the children has ceased, but the parents have carried hatred, anger and bitterness every day and every night since it happened. They have eaten, drunk, slept and dreamed of revenge against the perpetrators, one of whom has since died and the other is still in goal as I write this. The family members have been interviewed many times over the intervening thirty odd years. Raking over the old coals, building up and stoking the fires of hatred, and actually assisting them in making a totally self-destructive future for themselves, their nearest family, and all connected with them. That is a role they have chosen. Understandably, as in those days, there was nobody around to help them choose any other, and they have become those feelings now, and the beliefs those feelings engendered in them at the time. There were few councilors then to help them understand and accept their powerful feelings, and show them how to direct those feelings to other more productive ends. So instead of destroying just the children, the two sad, demented, criminally insane perpetrators also 'murdered' the parents and their families but, ironically, with the help of the parents and families themselves.

The Self-Help Delusion

Of course, we can never forget, but I am advocating forgiveness. What happened has happened, and all the hatred and vindictive bile in the world will not bring those children back. But hatred begets hatred, and all the newspaper reports over the years have incited the readers, who thrive on emotional revenge, to exercise that basic instinct. Until the day she died, the only picture of the woman involved was that printed in the papers, a police mug shot taken for the trial in 1967. That was just to make sure that the public did not forget or loose the anger and revulsion created by act, and epitomised by that picture at the time.

And that instinct for revenge is called up again and again by the media, not just against those guilty of this revolting crime, but those guilty of similar crimes against children and young people.

And revenge is not a useful emotion.

* * * * * * * *

On a more positive note, David Coulthard the F1 racing driver was involved in an airplane crash in May 2000. The private Lear jet had engine trouble, crash landed, burst into flames killing the pilot and the co-pilot. Coulthard, his girlfriend and his personal trainer scrambled out and walked away unscathed.

He said 'I should be dead now'; he was that close to being killed. You or I would be serious disturbed by that event. It would shake us to the degree that we might never fly again, and probably we would have a degree of post traumatic stress that would need some working through. But with Coulthard, no histrionics, no councilors, no recurring dreams, no PTSD. He lives his working life in the knowledge and full understanding that each day might be his last. So what's another close shave with death? The event has had little or no effect on him, because he does not attach the meaning to it that you or I would. His meaning seems to be 'I'm alive, get on with it'. For him, such events are all in a day's work. 72 hours later he was racing in the Spanish Grand Prix.

Communication – General

The quality of your life is determined by the quality of your communication.
Anthony Robbins

The quote above is one of my favorites.

Many people would define 'Communication' as when they talk to another person, face to face, or by telephone. When pushed they would include twitter, facebook, email, and snail mail (postage service). An even broader definition would include all forms of passing information to another, including singing, facial expression and body language. In line with this, I have the expression; 'You cannot not communicate'.

I have come to believe this is a useful realisation because it puts the responsibility for your communication directly on to you. Whenever you are in anyway in another's awareness, you are communicating. Whether you intend to or not, you are in some way affecting another's experience of you and their world.

That means (the meaning I give it.) that wherever you are and whatever you are doing, anyone who can experience you is receiving your communication.

To realise this helps one to be aware of the interrelatedness of all people, and the impossibility of not making a statement. The clothes you wear, the way you walk, your hairstyle, the way you look, the way you smile, the way you interact with friends and strangers.

All this communication intended or not, is a demonstration to yourself and a statement to the world about the sort of person you are choosing to be at that moment.

This might sound very fanciful, but what other reason is there for doing anything? In the end, that is what we are doing. Our communication is a demonstration to the world of who we are choosing to be. I guess you are not quite there with that one yet, but just take the idea on board for the duration of this chapter, and see how it goes.

It is significant to remember though, that we communicate in two directions, inward to ourselves and outwards to the world. Both processes are equally significant if we wish to enhance our level of contentedness.

Most people do not realise that what they communicate directly to themselves has far more significance to them than that which they communicate to others. You may think that you are only telling yourself what you already know and only putting it into words in order to structure it in your conscious mind. That is true, but it's only half the story.

Your unconscious mind is also listening to what your conscious mind is saying, and takes those directions when creating the events in your life. When you speak to another, there are four entities listening; your conscious and your unconscious mind, and also those of the other person. It's easy to neglect the communication you generate between one part of yourself and another. As you'll see, it is a vital part of the way we create our lives and the decisions we make about ourselves and others because it is this internal communication that your unconscious mind uses to create your life.

After all, who else do you think creates your life?

Inward Communication

One part of us is continually communicating with another part of us. Our observer that we spoke of in a previous chapter, the observer in our heads spends most of the time, especially when we are on our own, telling the computer of our mind what to do, how to do it, and what to think whilst doing it. It's vitally important that this communication is useful to us, and not destructive. We so often beat up on ourselves, over and over again, telling ourselves all sorts of negative things, telling ourselves the 'right' way to see a particular event, when in fact, that way is only one way to see it, and it may well not be a very useful way.

We touched on this in the last chapter when we looked at meaning, and what we make things mean to us.

I used to know someone at work who had a self-destructive internal dialog. David was full of energy, drive and enthusiasm, but persistently viewed many people as in some way out to get him. I couldn't write his actual words here, but he always felt that unless a person was within his inner circle of friends or colleagues, they were in some way potential enemies. An attitude of 'If you are not for me, you are against me'.

This is the approach so often espoused by the leaders of the USA I'm afraid. When you look at the shambles of their foreign policy, that half of the world dislikes them and the other half actually hate them, you can see that it's not an effective long term strategy to interact successfully with other people.

It's not that David's approach made him less effective, though in some ways it did, it's just that he spent a large proportion of his time and energy at work looking for the slight, the 'true' remark that showed the other person's 'real' feeling about him. And of course he found those remarks. You always can if you habitually interpret another's comments as though it were a slur on you personally. But it did prevent him from being transparent and open, and prevented him from having the simple, no special reason happiness that we all seek. I am very pleased to say that some three years later, working in a supportive environment and working with people who lovingly pointed out that there were other ways to see the world, his approach changed and he now sees all his relationships as I'm Ok, you're Ok and they're Ok too.

Another colleague, Annie was exactly the opposite. She saw all comments as good intentioned, and she had great difficulty seeing anything as a personal slur. She was open and direct, prepared to acknowledge her own shortcomings, and was tolerant of the shortcomings of others. She rarely needed to defend herself, because she almost never saw anything as an attack; except when it obviously was. When she did need to defend, she did so with perhaps an apology for her errors of understanding, a few facts to support her situation, and a hope that the other person would come back to her if they felt they needed to clear up the 'misunderstanding'. And her way was so much more effective for her own personal development and for the growth of the company. And she was so much happier with herself and the rest of the world.

These two outward behaviors perfectly reflect the inner communication that these two friends were unconsciously and consciously using.

This reminds me of a friend of about ten years who always seems to have a dragon in her life that needs slaying. It's almost as though she is looking for one, never fully happy until she's found one.

The realisation here is that she does look for them. We draw to us the people we need in order to demonstrate the personality we have created. In this case she needed an enemy to show to herself and the world who and what she is. She's the sort of person who 'stands up for herself', and who 'takes no shit from anyone' and she needs to demonstrate that. As I said earlier, I believe that's all we are doing, all of the time, we are demonstrating who we are.

* * * * * * * *

There might seem to be a conflict here between what I said earlier and what I've just said. Earlier I said that you are not your behavior, and now I am saying that you are.

One of the most useful realisations in life is that things are different dependant upon our point of view. That's not just a physical point of view but also an intellectual one. The way things are depends on how we look at them and where we are looking. Maybe we do need to demonstrate 'who we are' in this life, but that does not affect the 'who we really are' in the universal life. There are two things going on here. We have this life, where we show what we are choosing to be here, whilst still being what we really are in eternity; if you are into eternity.

So that's my meaning of life. To demonstrate the sort of person I want to experience being in this world; at this point in my life.

When I'm older I may decide to create a different personality. I know I can since, some time ago – like 25 years - I became tired

The Self-Help Delusion

of being a self-pitying wimp, and decided to change my approach to myself and the world. This book has become a reality because of that decision.

Remember in the chapter on meaning, we decide that nothing has meaning except the meaning you give it, and that's the meaning that I have chosen to give to my life. Not maybe the meaning given by other, notice, but in the here and now, it's my meaning. You can create any meaning you choose for your life.

* * * * * * * *

Having said that, let's look at what we say and who we are saying it to.

Following the model of the human being that makes the most sense to me, we have an unconscious mind, and it hears everything that we say, even though we say it to someone else, and it takes what we say personally. For instance, if we see someone dressed like a tart and driving a big black limousine, it's easy to think and to even say to yourself "Look at that cow. How did a woman looking like that ever get to own a car like that? She must be on the game or she's into drugs or crime of some sort". Your nconscious mind hears 'A car like that' 'on the game' 'Drugs' and 'Crime'. If your values prevent you from doing those things, then you will get no help from your unconscious mind in your aim to acquire a 'car like that'. Better to think and when talking to yourself to say, "That's a great car, and the lady driving it, she must have worked hard to bring a car like that into her life". The unconscious hears 'Work hard', 'Car like that'.

And since we are making it all up anyway, which though is the most useful to you? Your internal description of her is actually a description of you and the way you think of others, and that judgment of her doesn't damage her, but it does damage you.

Our thoughts affect what happens in our life. Thoughts are behaviors, and all behaviors lead to a different future. The trick is to choose behaviors that are the most useful to you rather than those that aren't. And in the above example, does it matter if the unconscious mind affects your future? Even if it doesn't, which of the above thoughts will cause you to be jealous, bitter and cynical, and which will help you to be positive and focused on creating your future to be the best it can be, given where you are at the moment in your life.

This is perhaps new thinking for you, you've never thought of it this way. Once you really get the idea that you are creating your life hour to hour, day to day, year by year with all you think and say and do, you will be creating it with volition and intent. After all, what or who else do you thing is doing the creating in your life?

* * * * * * *

There's another aspect of this inward communication that I think we could look at. At what point do we talk to another about something?

Thinking back to my comments about meaning, I think it can be more useful to give your unconscious mind time to find its own meaning rather than have the conscious mind jump to the first habit based meaning that presents itself in order to put the event into words and communicate it to your self and another. Once we have created the meaning for an event, putting it into words to communicate it sets that meaning in our minds, making it more difficult to change it later.

I remember being on a 20k charity walk a couple of years ago. After about an hour, I didn't feel particular well. My walking companion said 'how are you doing' and I replied, 'I don't know, I don't want to talk about it at the moment'. I didn't want to give the feeling meaning, in case I couldn't easily change it later on in the walk. I may have decided that it meant that I should quit, when in fact later I felt fine, and we completed the walk quite happily; tired but happy. I was actually quite pleased the way that my no longer young body handled 4 hours of walking, almost without a break.

Consciously not thinking or talking about something allows the unconscious mind to process it without giving it meaning at that time. Later the conscious mind can decide the meaning and allow you to consciously process it.

Outward communication

Words seem to be the main and obvious means of communication, so we'll start this topic with words. After all, words are the means that I am using to communicate with you now.

All words are metaphors. They are not an object or an event, a thought or a feeling, they only stand in place or represent to another, and indeed even to ourselves, our way of experiencing an object, event, thought or feeling. Each word is selected by each of us from a list of all the possibilities in our history (memory) in order (from our point of view) to best describe to another the way we see the world. Just as I am doing to you right now. I'll describe the process I'm now going through to communicate these ideas to you.

When I taught engineering, I used a lot of diagrams and pictures. Other people use music or movement to communicate an idea. In this situation, I'm using words to achieve that objective. The written work is the easiest form of communication to break down and to spot its basic components.

I search through my memory for a series of words or expressions that most closely express my thoughts or feelings to my satisfaction.

Using a word processor I arrange those words into well-formed sentences.

I add punctuation to better make sense, and conventional spelling to remove any ambiguity there might be, and italics and perhaps a capital letter to emphasise a word and give you an idea of its importance or significance to me in expressing the idea as exactly as I know how.

I read what I've written and try running the words and sentences, through my mind as though I were you, the reader, to make sure they express the ideas to my satisfaction, changing it where necessary until they do.

And that's my part done, and you take over.

What you do when you see a series of words on the page you read each word and search your memory for your meaning for each word. You hold the sentence in your mind. You then create a meaning that most closely fits your interpretation of the whole sentence and the whole paragraph.

You then believe that your meaning is my meaning and you re-act or respond to me with that meaning in your mind.

If you accept that the above is a very simplified way of thinking about the process of reading, writing - and listening for that matter - you might agree with another NLP idea, "Words don't have meanings, people have meanings for words."

If that's the case, then many of your domestic arguments are over the use of a word, are pointless because you make the fundamental mistake of thinking that when your partner or friends use the same word, you are talking about the same thing. And fundamentally you are, but many words have at least two levels of meaning.

There is the literal meaning and the emotional meaning.

There is usually little contention over the literal or given meaning of the proper nouns like table, bicycle, and chair, though these might have a secondary sentimental meaning. It's the abstract nouns we have a problem with as in 'One man's terrorist is another man's freedom fighter.'

The other meaning is the emotional meanings we attach to some words. Not all of course, but some.

I had a colleague called Chris. As I like to vary my language rather than sticking to the tried and tested, one day I called her Christine. Her re-action was immediate, and she shouted back at me across the office 'DO NOT CALL ME CHRISTINE'. Of course I realised I had touched a nerve and I walked over to her and in all seriousness, apologised. Softly I asked, "Did your father call you that (avoiding the name) when you were little". She smiled and said, "No, my mother when she was angry with me."

"Ok, I won't do it again" and we remained good friends.

There's a lesson here. Hers was a re-action, coming from her history, not a response from the here and now, and also the re-action had nothing to do with me. I could not have known the additional meaning she had for her name and she would have responded that way whoever had called her Christine. Or maybe it was a compliment to me as she unconsciously knew she could get away with an outburst directed at me, but not necessarily at another of her colleagues.

The Self-Help Delusion

(Notice the meaning I chose to give her 'unreasonable' re-action. I didn't see it as a personal slur to me, but a compliment to me that she knew I would not get annoyed at her outburst whereas others might.)

Of course, had I re-acted with emotion rather than responding with understanding, the long term outcome could well have been different.

So with the literal meaning, the dictionary gives the 'official' meaning, and generally that is a good place to start, depending on how old the dictionary is. Many words now are given different meanings to those generally accepted in the past. The words 'gay' for example, and 'wicked' and 'cool' have taken on totally different additional meanings. In others, the dictionary meaning may be the same, but associations have changed. Older people may still cling to the associations that they learned as a child, and younger people have acquired their own.

Some time ago my sister was once describing the way the government agency she worked for communicates to its staff. She was saying that the agency talks about 'business units' and 'customers'. "But it's all nonsense", she protested, "We are not a business. It cannot be a 'business', as there is no profit, and the 'customers' we provide the services for are not 'customers', as they have no choice but to do as the law prescribes they do."

We spent half an hour arguing about this but then I learned and now I realise that we were arguing over the meaning of a word, and words don't have meanings anyway.

The word 'customer' now includes anyone to whom you provide goods or services, either external to or within your own organisation. Good business practice considers internal customers just as important as external ones, and a 'business' can be any group of people that provides those goods and services.

My definition matches today's definition of 'business', and 'customers' which is far broader than the one my sister had affixed in her head, set firmly in her formative years, and which she never changed. This didn't make me 'right' and her 'wrong' but I does show the different ways in which we think of the ideas behind the words.

Peter Seal

* * * * * * *

When you use a word, you have two reasons for choosing it. One, because it provides the primary meaning you wish to convey, and two, because it 'feels right' to you when you say it to yourself. You select that word out of all the other possibilities because of the way you feel about it. And that feeling is yours, and nobody else's.

We all use the word 'divorce', and we all know legally what it means, but the underlying connotations carried by that word can be very different with different people. If you are sixty years old, from a middle class family, with some Sunday school experiences, it's likely that divorce would be tantamount to impossible for you. There are too many taboos surrounding it, and to many strictures from your past. "Other people can divorce, but people like me do not". You could never see yourself as a divorcee.

On the other hand, if you are a twenty two year old female, with little or no religious belief, and married at eighteen to someone who had plenty between his legs but nothing between his ears, you would be less likely to see divorce as a sign of moral degeneracy, and think it a perfectly viable alternative to being stuck with this wastrel all your life.

It really does depend on where you are coming from as to the secondary meaning you attach to words.

It's sad really, how we have a meaning for a word, and then steadfastly refuse to change that meaning, even when it becomes very clear that the person we are using it to communicate with does not hold our meaning for it. Because it's a word, with a dictionary definition, we mistakenly believe we are right in our meaning for it, when in fact there is no 'right' meaning for it. We only find alternative 'right' meanings when we are misunderstood. Then we have to find a word whose meaning we can agree on, or change our meaning for it in the light of another's thoughts and comments.

This concept is very obvious when we play charades, and the group does not grasp the meaning we are trying to communicate. We don't just do the same thing over and over again in the hope that the audience changes their understandings. We change what

The Self-Help Delusion

we do until we can find a way to communicate our meaning. In fact, if you watch carefully, having failed to communicate their meaning, the communicator will often actually stop what they are doing, drop their arms to their sides to indicate a change of direction, and you can 'see' them thinking - 'what else can I do, how are this group interpreting what I've done already, perhaps if I take this approach they will understand', and then they begin again with an alternative strategy.

We are blessed with words but also their victims. With words, because we think they have a meaning that everyone knows and agrees with, we tend to keep on re-iterating the same words and sentences in an attempt to get this 'stupid' person to understand. And that strategy does not work. You don't change the meaning someone has for a word by saying it again, or even louder. You have to use different words, a different context and different sentences. Or you have to explain to them your meaning for the word, and use one of their words that mean to them what your word means to you. And then, when you are getting back the responses that tell you that you are understood, you can begin to move on to the next part of your communication.

One of the presuppositions of NLP is "The meaning of your communication is the response you get". That is to say, when you communicate, in this case verbally, the meaning of your communication to that person is not maybe the meaning you had in your head when you generated the words, but it is shown in the way the receiver reacts/responds to your communication because that is what it means to them.

Their response may be unfair, it may be irrational, it may be an over the top physical reaction to an innocent phrase or expression, as with my work colleague Chris, but that's what your communication means to them from where they are at that point in their state of mind and history.

We decide our meaning for a word when we first hear it, and some will never change their meaning for it, even when the world does.

If however the other person says something that matches your thoughts, their meaning may not be that far from your own, and you will be of like mind - maybe.

How much more effective would communication be if both parties espoused these realities. But old habits die hard. We just do what the English have always done with foreigners, raise our voice and gesticulate a lot.

An appreciation of all this stuff will help in reducing the frustration that we can experience when another does not understand what we want or feel, and also helps us to be more understanding of the real situation rather than just saying, or at least feeling, 'are you stupid or something?'

So, this leaves us with the realisation that we are 100% responsible for the effectiveness of our communication.

The responsibility lies with you to ensure that whatever you want to communicate has been communicated effectively. If the response you get is not the one you want then you need to try other words, other sentences, backtrack, re-enforce, re-iterate and anything else that will get you the response you want.

* * * * * * *

These days we are inundated with the concept of Political Correctness or PC. As I understand it, the idea is that we must never say anything at which another could take offence. This is clearly impossible as the sender of the message has no control over the interpretation that another might put on that message.

PC I think was a logical follow on from the new-age culture that began to hit some time in the late seventies. Some people make a career, and ultimately a life out of taking offence at what other people and organisations might communicate to them. They then threaten the organisation with the law which settles out of court to save embarrassment. Small claims; £10,000 is a reasonable payoff from a large organisation. It is a big band wagon, and lots of people are jumping on it. We are so sensitive to PC and 'isms (Racism, Sexism and now Ageism) that if someone chooses to use any of these as an excuse for incompetence, it is difficult to refute it. I have come across employees who were clearly incompetent at their job,

The Self-Help Delusion

and when dismissed, claimed an 'ism as the reason. It's very non PC to simply say, 'it's not because you are female / black / Irish / Muslim / old that you have been sacked, it's because you are incompetent, and show no signs of wanting not to be.

As you read that sentence, you may think me a racist, and that thought is as a result of the promotion of PC concepts that we have all been subject to in the last thirty odd years.

Racism or any other 'ism' is about intent and meaning. It's the ultimate generalisation.

To me, a more practical approach to the situation than the PC lobby provide is one of Political Sensitivity - PS, where we bear in mind the sensitivity of our audience, and communicate to where they are, not to where we think they should be. It is clearly insensitive to refer to a black person as a Nigger, unless you are a black person yourself when it seems to be acceptable. It has unpleasant, absolutely valid, connotations in history of the slave trade and abuse of the black man. (better add 'and black woman', in case a reader might think I'm being sexist!)

On the other hand, to avoid using words in contexts where they have always been used – Blackball, Blackmail, Manhole, Whitewash etc, seems to me to pander to the learned sensitivities of others.

I've heard recently about offence kleptomaniacs. Whenever they see a possible offence lying around, they can't help picking it up and running with it.

A friend and colleague of mine, Angela, an African woman was offended by being called 'coloured' by a work colleague. When Angela expressed her annoyance, the colleague, instead of apologising, tried to suggest that she shouldn't be offended – not a good idea - and she succeeded in digging herself into an even deeper hole. Of course, all she was trying to do was to avoid the word 'black' as PC has been telling us, and succeeded only in causing even more offence by using the word 'coloured' Sometimes it's difficult to win.

Naturally, and in keeping with all that's in this book, if offence has been caused, then apologise with sincerity, realising that the meaning of the communication to the recipient was the response you got, and then change what you say with the aim of getting the response you do want. The apology that is worded 'I'm sorry for any offence I may have caused' is yet another insult, as the offence was caused, not may have been.

PC however has caused us to think of words, and their deeper meaning and NLP provides the realisation that the words we select describe the way we think about things. Take the word 'lazy'. If a mother describes her 10 year old son as 'lazy', then in her mind she has put him in a box with the label of 'Lazy' on the outside, as though that were an unchangeable statement of fact. Like a box in the supermarket with 'Lager' on the outside. That's it. And in the same way that a can of lager is a can of lager, there's nothing she can do about her son being lazy.

When she labels her son as lazy it gives him the same unchanging status as the box of lager. And that's not useful. Her son is a process, not a fixed entity. He is becoming an adult, and adults are becoming older adults. Dr Wayne Dyer said, "I'm not a human being, I'm a human becoming.", and to my clients, I use the expression, "You are a work in progress, not a fixed entity".

Rather than describe someone as 'lazy', it's more useful to use the word 'unmotivated'. This might sound very 'new-ageist' but it gives the mother the opportunity and even the responsibility to find out what does motivate him, and use that knowledge to encourage him to change his behaviors to those that will be more useful to him as he moves through life. Telling him to 'Shift your ass.' or 'do your homework.' or whatever, is not going to motivate him, because the trick to motivation is to realise that people only ever do things for themselves, and at this point, he sees no personal advantage to 'shift his ass' or 'do his homework'.

Throughout this book I have avoid the use of the words 'good' and 'bad' and right' and 'wrong'.

This is done intentionally. These words label things from my perspective, and that may well not be your perspective. I cannot motivate you from my perspective; you can only be motivated from yours. Those words separate people. Your 'right' might not be my 'right' and a resistance to what you are saying builds in my mind, even as you are saying it. So I use the word 'useful' a lot because that then allows you to work out if the ideas we are talking about or the beliefs presented in your reading will be of use to you, given what you want to achieve in your life. Then you will know what activities will assist you in achieving your objectives. I'm not into telling people what to do. Provide people with a choice - an awareness of their options - and they will exercise their power to choose.

The underlying arc in this book is to increase your choices in life, and to reduce the control or power that you give to others.

I want you to have choices and to feel empowered because when you are, you can make decisions and follow through with useful actions. It's not that you feel dis-empowered; you just don't feel empowered to make choices where you don't see any choices.

Before we move on, let's look at the word 'problem', and I offer you a question. 'Would we still have problems if we didn't have the word problem?

The obvious answer is yes. We think of a problem as something to be overcome, to be tackled, to be fought. The 'war on drugs' is a good example; something to be fought against, an enemy stopping you achieving your goal. For most people there is a whole series of negative feelings attached to the word 'problem'

I don't think that the negative connotations that, for many people surround the word are useful emotions connected with achieving the goal

There is a quotation, 'Part of the problem is the way you see the problem'. If we look at the situation that the word problem is used to describe, it is only a series of undesirable events or circumstances. That's all. There is nothing to fight, nothing to overcome, nothing to feel negative about. There is just an action required, or series of actions, that will change the events or circumstances to those we want.

The media and politicians do not see it that way. They believe that just changing the word doesn't change the way people think about something. But when we spoke of lazy earlier, that word described the way we think of someone, and that by changing it to 'unmotivated', we can think of the person and their actions in a very different and more useful way.

Part of the problem is the way you see the problem. Modern management has us think about problems as challenges or opportunities.

I know that it can be very irritating at times. I once had a manager who spoke like that. When fresh excrement was about to hit the fan, he would say '… just consider this a window of opportunity Peter.' Not very helpful in the circumstances though I suppose he was right in some ways, because in overcoming the problem, or 'devising a course of action to eliminate the adverse situation', to use new-age speak, I suppose I learned something.

I also note that sales people, having done some additional service – perhaps put your purchases in a bag - will reply to your 'thanks' with 'No problem'. I suppose it helps to take the negative connotations from the word though why mention a problem when there isn't one. Much better to smile and say 'My pleasure'

Communication - Tools

In the technical process of verbal communication, there several techniques available to us. They are what I call the tools of communication. I call them tools as they are devices to assist us in achieving our conversational objectives.

When we communicate to another person by the use of words and sentences, the way we do it has been analysed, and there are six processes or tools that all people use.

Meta comments
I'll start by taking a look at Meta comments.

Meta comments are when it is the secondary message that is responded to, not the primary message. Earlier, in the chapter on choice, we looked at what we might say if your friend is criticising your mother. You would feel the temptation to become angry as your loyalty to your mother is being put to the test.

The **primary** message is the content of what is said.

The **secondary** message is the driving emotion that is causing it to be said, at that time and in that manner.

The Primary message is the criticism of your mother's behavior.

The secondary message is some frustration or anger, seemingly at her, but really about something or someone else.

The emotion for all criticism comes from fear of something – often having no connection to the content or the person or event or object being criticised or to whom the anger is directed. The 'Christine' incident mentioned earlier is a good example. And although it is often not easy to determine the real cause of the fear – feelings of impending loss, vulnerability, anger, inadequacy, frustration, jealousy or whatever, it's not necessary to know the reason at this level. Any response that tries to get past the primary message (the content) and addresses the secondary message (the feelings of anger, frustration, fear or whatever) will allow the conversation to flow and develop. Often apologies will follow, when the other person realises or is prepared to acknowledge the underlying driving thought that prompted their comments in the first place.

In the above situation, it is more useful to respond to the secondary message – the cause of the comments, rather than the primary message – the content about your mother and this response is a meta-comment on the feelings that prompted the remarks, not on the content of the remark.

As I said then, you could attack him for insulting your mother. That's the primary message. It is far better to respond to the secondary message and say something like 'Yes, I can see why you see it that way, but let's move on.' What have you planned for the weekend.' or 'God Tony, you are pissed off this morning (with a laugh), what's bugging you. It isn't John again is it?' or something similar which suits your style.

This manner of response gets straight to a person. It doesn't just say 'I understand how you feel' it demonstrates that you understand how he feels. You have bypassed the content, and accessed the feelings that prompted the comments. Most often this is the most effective response if continued harmony is your objective.

There are occasions when it is useful to pick the primary message to respond to, and sometimes the secondary. I had an example of that recently when I took over a job from someone who had resigned, and I had three days with her to get an overview of the job. She was frustrated at the company, and I suspect with her life, and she was not easy to get on with. She was abrupt, aggressive and short tempered, but I consciously ignored her emotion, and concentrated on what it was she was telling me. It was strange, because towards the end of the second day, she became easier and friendlier. Some part of her realised that I was not responding to her anger and frustration, and she had just about dropped it when our time together ended, because she realised that her feelings were nothing to do with me, and I was simply not going to feel affronted or take offence at her comments.

I suppose if I'd had to work with her for any length of time

I would have listened to her frustrations and anger and perhaps empathise with her situation. We could then at least have had an easier relationship but in the three days I had, I would not have found out anything about the job I was about to take over. She might have unloaded her thoughts to me, but in the time I had, nothing much would have changed in her.

It is your responsibility to decide, in a given conversation, which of the messages you are receiving; whether it is more useful to respond to the primary message or to the secondary message. Decide what you want to achieve and concentrate on the message that will help you to achieve your objective for that communication.

* * * * * * *

Disclosures
The next tool I'd like to look at is 'Disclosures'. Disclosures are used to build rapport with another person. A disclosure is when you give something of yourself to another. You tell them something about yourself.

The significance of a disclosure can range from a fairly inconsequential fact, which you could say to almost anyone, like, 'I was born in London' to something which puts you at risk in some way, either feelings of which you are a little ashamed, or some fact about you or your history that you would rather be different.

Disclosures are a very useful tool for getting to know people beyond the superficial level.

The general rule is that we each contribute to a conversation in turn, and your disclosure generates the rapport with your conversation partner that will tend to lead them to follow with a disclosure of their own.

Of course, we have all known people who are very difficult to 'get to know', and a little understanding of disclosures shows why.

I used to run a postage stamp shop, and I got to know my customers in varying degrees of intimacy – as you would expect. One man I knew for about five years. He would come in perhaps three times a week, and we would go to the cafe along the end of the road and have tea and muffins. On one or two days each week he would buy sandwiches and come home with me for lunch. That happened on and off for about four years. Then he moved home a little later and we lost contact. The point is, I knew him no better at the end of our five year relationship than I did after the first five weeks. He disclosed nothing of himself.

I gave my disclosures, but he returned none; plenty of facts, and opinions and detail, but no feelings, nothing risky. I think our relationship was the poorer for that, but that was the way he needed it to be at that time in his life, so OK, what the hell, he was my friend and a sounding board for my ideas, and he taught me a lot about stamps and postal history, so it worked for us both I guess. But I never got close, because without disclosures, the real person is never revealed.

I knew another man, who came from the north of England, as I do, and within five minutes of meeting him, we were past the trivial, and we were, what I now realise is 'disclosing' away, and building mutual trust and respect. Perhaps it was because we both came from the north of England. People there tend to be more open and direct. We never became social friends, but it was a simple honest open relationship, which we both enjoyed.

Disclosures build empathy and trust. To be trusted with details about someone makes it easier to trust them in return.

On the other hand, gushing disclosures can be embarrassing. Meeting someone for the first time, there is a depth of intimacy that seems 'normal', and beyond that, it can be difficult to feel comfortable. 'Why is she telling me all this stuff?' 'Does she expect me to do something about it?' and 'Why me?' are natural internal responses to gushing disclosures. Gushing disclosures can also lead to disclosure remorse. This is where one person has so much bottled inside them that given a willing ear, they remove the cork. Problem is that the following day or week, the person is so embarrassed at having disclosed so much that they avoid meeting you again. I have lost at least three potential friends that way.

The simple rule is, give one or two disclosures, and see if any are returned. If not, give up at that point, and try again later in the conversation. How 'friendly' the person is will be apparent from their response to your disclosures. Those who follow your lead, and disclose themselves in turn, will lead you to feel good, that you 'got on well' and that there could be some future in the relationship, whatever its objectives.

Recently I was at a cheese and wine party at a friend's house. Most people were in the same social set as the group. A man and his wife and a young toddler were there and seemingly on their own, so I started to chat to the husband. I got nowhere. I told him something about myself. Nothing. I told him something else about my family and asked a relevant question. Still nothing. I spoke with his wife about their child and other than a polite reply, still nothing. I hung around for a short time, and then moved away to the group that I did know. Normally I am successful in getting to know strangers. I realised of course that his lack of spontaneity or friendliness was nothing to do with me. That's where he was in his mind at that time, and that's ok. There could be all sorts of reasons for it but I'm not given to fabricating reasons.

The bottom line is that, used with sensitivity and discretion, disclosures build relationships.

* * * * * * *

Reflections

The next tool is called Reflections and again it's used to build rapport.

I'll give you my definition. A reflection is when you paraphrase what the other person says, where possible **using the same words, expressions and phrases that they use**. You reflect back to the other person, a consolidated version of what they have said. This leads them to believe that you understand what they are talking about; that you are thinking and feeling exactly what they are thinking and feeling and hence you build and maintain a rapport with that person.

Now this might seem to be a manipulative move. And of course it can be if you have selfish intentions. In passing here, a little on the expressions 'influencing', and 'manipulating'

There is a wonderful book called 'Influencing with Integrity' (see bibliography) and with all communication you 'should' never seek to manipulate the other person through tricks of speech, or knowledge of techniques. To me the difference between manipulation and influencing is quite clear. Manipulating is when you seek to take from the other person - you win and they loose. Influencing is when you aim to assist another and yourself to achieve your joint objectives - you win and they win.

My intention in writing this book is to influence you and assist you in creating a more fulfilling life for yourself and those you love. I'm guessing that's what you want, or you would not have picked up the book in the first place.

If they are the looser by any of your communication, it was manipulation. If they gain from the conversation, then it was influencing.

If you manipulate another person, you are both the loser. You know it right away, and then you will have to justify yourself to yourself at some point in time. The other party will realise after a time that they have been manipulated, and the relationship will be the worse for it.

I know one man who is a manipulator. He has studied NLP, and uses his knowledge and skills in order to manipulate people and circumstances. I think he believes that is the way to happiness, but judging from his track record, it doesn't seem to be working. I don't know a single person who trusts him. The pity is, he doesn't know what he is doing wrong. He has a belief that he has to win, and because of this, he always looses.

That is often the case in life. People tend to do something to achieve a desired end, and when it doesn't, they do the same thing only harder. Only after a long time, if ever, do they realise, and try something different. Some people die before they realise that what they are doing will not achieve for them what they will for themselves; sad really.

* * * * * * * *

Interpretations

The next tool is 'Interpretations'. Interpretations are opposite to disclosures and reflections in that they are used as a tool to create understanding, not to build rapport.

When you are attempting to understand what the other person really means you will use interpretations and you will paraphrase what the other person says where possible **using your own words, expressions and phrases**.

This means that you have absorbed what the other person has said, and then re-created the thoughts, ideas etc, using your own words, whose meaning is very clear to you, and then pass that to the other person to let them re-create their meaning from your words and then compare that meaning with their original meaning. Any discreparency between what they mean and what they realise you think they mean will be apparent to them, and they will correct those discreparencies and change their words to be closer to yours. You then both begin again. When you have a form of words that you are both happy with, when there are no discreparencies, if you ever get to that state – you will have transferred your meaning to another, and they to you.

People do that instinctively. We have not been taught to do that, it just happens; but actually not often enough. Communication is an exact science, but because we all do it, it is assumed that we all do it well, and that is simply not the case. Most people are poor communicators in that they think that when they have said their bit, that their job over.

To sum up, we use their words to create rapport, and your own words to gain understanding.

* * * * * * * *

Advisements

Advisements are used where we believe our view of their situation would be useful to the other person, and we say so. For example: when we mention that we enjoyed a particular book or film and that they might enjoy it too: recommending your dentist as being gentle and thoughtful, suggesting how to cook a particular meal, and not to overcook the vegetables, suggesting one specific course of action rather than another. In fact, as I am doing for you in this book.

This book is actually a series of advisements. The above are all examples of advisements. We spend half our life advising people what to do and how to do it.

Unfortunately, much of the advising ends up with the adviser having the power in the relationship. The psychological need some people have to hold the power in a relationship can cause them to give more than minimum advisements. Advisements can be a useful tool for creating rapport and assisting someone else achieve their aims, but if overused, it is like running another person's life for them.

Some people tell you what to do, when to start, when to stop, how to do it, and what to think whilst you're doing it. It becomes interference in another's life, and that can lead to all parties being worse off. It can create an inferiority complex, a lack of trust in their own judgment by the person being advised, even anger at being discounted, and that creates a resentment of the person doing the advising. Discretionary use is useful, overuse is counter-productive.

* * * * * * *

Questions

The next tool is 'Questions'. Questions are asked by one party to elicit more information, or in a more subtitle form, to help the other person to realise something that they may have known already, but hadn't understood.

It's easy to see the process as one person asks a question, another person answers it. That's all.

What questions always do is to cause people to think. The questions I ask you in these pages are intended to have you realise – make real - what you already feel and know about a subject.

I used to be a college lecturer a long time ago, teaching physics and maths among other things. Part of my technique was to see how little I had to actually tell the students once we were past the basics in a topic. If the questions are well structured, and the desired answer already known by the questioner, then many people do not need to be told the answer. By a process of small discrete steps the student can be lead to the answer almost by themselves. They could have done it without the teacher, the knowledge was inside them, and they just hadn't found the path to it because they hadn't asked themselves the necessary questions in the necessary order. Many research workers invent and discover by asking themselves the questions: What if, Why, When, Where and How. There is nobody to give them the answers, because nobody 'knows', but the process will lead them to answers they had never dreamt of.

Einstein realised his theory of relativity by asking himself the question, 'what would the world look like if I could travel on a beam of light'. His theory of relativity started in his head. He then went on to prove it mathematically.

The question is a vital device to enable us to understand and is all important to both the asker and the asked. There is a whole study around the form a question might take, but here is not the place for such a discussion.

* * * * * * *

Silence
The last conversational tool is 'Silence'.

Silence is the gap in the conversations where usually, neither party knows what to say next. This can be quite embarrassing, especially if you don't know the other person very well.

Silences can be used to give people time to structure their thoughts and feelings, especially their feelings.

Silence – saying nothing - can be used as a manipulative device, as the power is with the person who doesn't break the silence. Ask a question and say nothing. The other person will answer it. If you still say nothing, he will feel obligated to continue. Still say nothing, and he will continue, and may well say far more that he had intended to and give away far more of himself. This gives the questioner power if he chooses to use it. That is how the police and interrogators work. Create a menacing environment, ask a question and still say nothing, even after the first question is answered. The suspect will feel the need to give a more complete answer when the first one doesn't seem to satisfy the questioner.

Freudians use the same technique in psycho analysis, where the client has to dig deeper to find an answer to satisfy the practitioner.

Some time ago I was working in an emotionally charged environment, and we were given counseling in order to help us unwind. My first session with a new councilor didn't go too well, as I knew exactly what she was trying to do, and I refused to co-operate. I think it annoyed me to think that she thought I was so easy to 'play'. We sat and looked at each other for about five minutes before she realised that I wasn't going to play her game, honesty broke out, and she stopped playing councilor. Not being a councilor, I didn't really have much stuff to unload anyway.

Used in a non manipulative way, in say a therapeutic situation, the client will verbalise some of the 'stuff' in their unconscious mind and bring it out into the open for examination by the conscious mind, and that is the beginnings of their recovery. They need the silence to formulate into the conscious mind what is actually in the unconscious mind, and the time, space, freedom and safety to do it.

The Origin of Belief

Our beliefs are what drive us. Beliefs are what caused the Cold War for 35 years. Beliefs are what caused the holocaust, killing 6 million people. Beliefs are what caused the Vietnam War. Beliefs are what took Mother Theresa to Calcutta. The world is changed by the beliefs of those in power or those seeking to obtain power. Beliefs created the Channel Tunnel, and the Empire State building. Beliefs are the driving force of our world. We function in thought and word and deed. Your thoughts are reflections of your beliefs, and your words and actions follow. Each one of us creates our world through our beliefs.

A useful belief is that beliefs are a choice. We can pick and choose them as we will. This is obviously within reason. I might tell myself that the sun is made of cream cheese, but that belief is difficult to sustain given our knowledge about the temperature of the sun and the melting point of cheese. Metaphorically, it makes the point that beliefs cannot be irrational, but oddly, they can

My late sister had a belief – in spite of all the warnings - that smoking 40 Capstan Full strength cigarettes every day wouldn't do her any harm. Nothing I could say or do had any effect on this belief, and sadly, although her mother had lived to 93. My sister died a physical wreck at 71. Beliefs are dangerous things when based to ignorance, habit and certainty.

Now I don't know if we can choose our beliefs or not, but I have changed far more in the fifteen or so years believing it and acting as if it were true than ever I did in the 50 years before.

It is better to believe something useful to us than to stick with old beliefs that are taking us nowhere, and hold us back in the past. If my sister had examined her beliefs about smoking – given all the research in the last 20 years - she would be alive and well today.

So, add the belief that beliefs are a choice. Give it a whirl for a time. Decide what beliefs would be useful and start acting as though they were true. After all, one way to change our behavior is to change our beliefs, and one way to change our beliefs is to change our behavior. I'm not saying that any of this is easy; it's not, because our beliefs are one of the ways we define ourselves to ourselves. And if we change or add a new belief, we will no longer be the person we are now, but we will have a choice as to which belief to cling to and behave as though it were true. And choice is about empowerment.

Some people are strongly against change, and struggle against changing themselves. It can be scary. It's easier to stick with what and who we believe we are, rather than to change to the unknown. Better the known self than the unknown self. However, to change our behavior in the long term, easily and unconsciously, we have to change our beliefs. If a person tries consciously to say, stop smoking, and their unconscious mind is not in agreement, then they will not be able to. Those people who have stopped easily had an unconscious mind that wasn't bothered one way or another.

* * * * * * *

Let's look at how we acquire or form our beliefs in the first place.

Inculcation
When we are children, we have our beliefs thrust upon us. Sometimes, on Sunday mornings, down our street, I see families with the husband in a business suit and a well dressed wife, each with an attaché case and often accompanied by a child. They are Jehovah's Witnesses, and just one of many religious people trying to catch the malleable mind of the young, before the attractions of the world have their influences. The parents obviously believe that their way of life is the way to a happy life, and want their children to benefit from their experience.

That child is inculcated with the beliefs of whatever concepts of right / wrong that that particular religion expounds. Religion, subsumed into a culture is a hard taskmaster and militates against

The Self-Help Delusion

later change. 'Catholic guilt' being a major handicap to happiness - in my opinion.

There are three major forces or areas of belief in any society; politics, religion and the physical forces of police or army. When these three forces – or beliefs - are controlled by one group of people, that society is going nowhere. Those societies who have these beliefs held separately are the ones who have developed the world for the good of the majority of their people. Those societies that have these beliefs held by one group have done very little for their people in the last 1000 years. If you doubt these beliefs, look around in the world, now and in history.

Continuous experience

I believe in gravity. It makes things fall down. I've seen the effects of gravity all my life. When I was young, I didn't think about it, or think there could any other way that teacups and teddies and toast could behave other than fall to the floor when there was nothing underneath to hold them up. I really do believe in gravity because I fall as well if there is nothing under me; every time, without fail. Just when I've forgotten about gravity, there it is again, ouch, reminding me that it is still there.

One off experience

A phobia is an irrational fear and often created with only one experience. Human beings are very fast learners on occasions. When a child, being trapped in a cupboard or falling into water or 'playfully' being taken to the edge of a cliff or onto the edge of a flat roof, all these events are given a meaning of danger, and the belief of danger is created.

In adulthood, these fears may be difficult to overcome. Sometimes that belief does not reduce the quality of life, and so we don't bother to work on fixing it. If it's a severe phobia, it can inhibit your enjoyment of a normal life.

My wife has a fear of mice, or indeed, almost any animal smaller than a cat. She cannot even be in the same room as a mouse, even a dead one. What harm she rationally thinks a dead mouse is going to do her I'm not sure, but all the reasoning in the world does not take away her fear. I guess something happened to her as a child, and her unconscious mind created a fear, and she still has it. That is a phobia, because her fear is disproportionate to the current danger.

That's the way phobias work. A belief was created at a time when there may have been a good reason for the associated emotion, but carried through to the here and now, where the emotion is grossly out of proportion to the actual reason for the emotion. A fear of mice and spiders is a good example.

My daughter has a phobia of fungus. She has difficulty walking through a wood in the late summer / autumn time when she can smell them. I think I may have created that fear by throwing fungus at her, just for fun, when she was a little child. I remember doing it, but of course I didn't know the possible implications that it might bring about. I forgive myself for doing that for as the bible says, 'Lord, forgive them, for they know not what they do'.

Explanation
If we come back to gravity again, we know that things fall down, given a chance. How does that explain the earth, the moon, the planets and the solar system as a whole?

Isaac Newton realised, or devised or discovered the law of gravity, which he said controls the movement of the moon around the earth, and the planets around the sun. That was around 1670. People believed that Newton's laws of gravity explained the movements of the solar objects, and even the tides on earth. It just seems a pretty solid explanation, and was totally accepted by the scientific community, as all the measurements they could make with the instruments of the time confirmed the laws

It took until the turn of the twentieth century for Albert Einstein to prove that Newton was right in principle, but wrong in his basic concepts. We still use Newton's laws of motion when designing mechanical devices today because at the velocities and forces on earth, the results are 'near enough', but they are useless when we try and explain quantum mechanics

Example
Religion relies on the process of example. I've not physically seen

The Self-Help Delusion

God, nor felt him, nor tasted him, nor used any of my five senses to 'know' he exists. Something deep inside 'knows' he does, and in moments of crisis, people will often pray to a God they had never given a second thought to since they were a child. The belief may well not be recognised, but it is still there and (like gravity) it becomes apparent sometimes and surprises us. But because it's there, our behavior is affected by it.

Fear
During the first world war they used to say, 'there are no atheists in the trenches' and firm beliefs come out in times of adversity. We have construct beliefs about everything. Dogs cannot be trusted. Policemen can be trusted. All mothers love their children. I cannot do that. He makes me angry. That's not fair; thousands of little beliefs that we have acquired, or adopted or copied as we have created our lives all our lives. Some of these beliefs serve us, some of them are obviously true, some are generalisations, and some are false. Some are true up to the time you realise they aren't. Some were given to us when we were too young to know any different. Some we grasped in pain, as a drowning man does a straw, in an attempt to teach ourselves something in order to avoid feeling that pain or suffering again. Every time you express your opinion, you are describing your belief. Every time you make any judgment or criticism you are expressing a belief. Our conversations are peppered with beliefs. Every prejudice is a belief, every comment comes from a belief that it is the way that it is, and must be the way we see it. Most of our 'facts' are really beliefs. How do we know whatever? 'I read it in the paper'. And that makes it true does it? I don't think so. The world is as full of falsehoods now as it ever was, but more people can read them now than ever before, and they create their beliefs from their experiences, as do we all.

Examine your beliefs. Decide which ones serve you, and discard the ones that don't. Do not try and work out which are true. You obviously think they are all true otherwise you would have given up on the untrue ones a long time ago. Remember: This book is about what works, not about what you consider to be true.

So we are back again to the 'whatever works'. Never mind if it is true. Don't waste your time looking for the truth. There are plenty of people and organisations that will tell you what the truth is. Problem is, they all have different truths. Generally when someone says 'well, the truth is…' I think to myself, well, it my be your truth, but it's perhaps not mine.'

* * * * * * *

Do you want to change a belief you have, one that doesn't assist you to a happy life?

When you say something or do something, stop and ask yourself, what do I believe that caused me to say / do that? Only by asking yourself the question will you find out what you believe.

Take the belief that is holding you back, stopping you doing something that you want to do, and consider it false. Acquired long ago perhaps, in a time of stress perhaps, in a time of pain, perhaps, at a time when your discriminating faculties were not what they are now. Create a new belief; one that serves you. You don't believe it now, but give it a try. Act as though it were true. Try it on for size for a while.

* * * * * * *

Perhaps you would like to be a writer. For me, a writer is someone who writes, whereas an author is someone who has had writings published. Perhaps you don't see yourself as a writer. But then you won't if you don't write. If you write, you are by definition, 'a writer'. You may not have had anything published as yet, so redefine yourself in the light of the fact that you are a writer but not yet an author.

You see what I mean? All you need to do is change your definition of 'a writer' and then write something.

You are a writer who has not as yet had anything published. Now that gives you the freedom to write as a writer, not as a non-writer. And freedom comes with that confidence, and the open-heartedness to do the actions that will make you an author.

It's only a limiting belief that is stopping you. And you no doubt have other beliefs about 'writers' as well. Writers need a degree in English – not true. Writers need to have time to write – not true, make time, even an hour a day. Writers need a broad vocabulary – untrue, it depends on your audience. Writers are born not made – untrue, many authors did not write until their 50's. You have absolutely no current evidence to support all these beliefs. You may have been told when you were in infant's class that your spelling was rubbish, or your vocabulary was poor, or that you couldn't string two words together effectively, and bingo, a belief was created. And in order to support that belief, you created all the other beliefs too. You still had those beliefs right the way up to now. And that is what stopped you becoming a writer; nothing else.

That old belief came to limit you – how could you be a writer? And you can now think, why not. I have a quick mind, I have the vocabulary, I have the ability to read a sentence and know when it scans, I have a computer to make it easy, and I have something significant to say. So what's the problem?

Go for it.
Beliefs are the story we tell ourselves is true. A significant event occurs, and we create a story – give it meaning – in order never to forget it. And we don't forget it. And each time the event occurs now, we remember the story, and hence we say 'No, I can't do that because…' and then tell ourselves the story that we told ourselves at the time the event first happened.

Beliefs are the rules by which we run our life. Many were handed to us when we were very young. Many are no longer relevant. Many are completely irrational. Many have no evidence to support them.

* * * * * * *

Sometimes I use the word 'know' and sometimes 'believe'. For me there are two separate relationships between myself and whatever the topic to know or believe. If we were to put each of those relationships in separate boxes, one marked 'know' and the other marked 'believe' then most people would put the 'know' box inside the 'believe' box, in that how can they possibly know it if they don't believe it. Most people would say that one can't know something one doesn't believe. The knowing is encompassed by the original belief.

I don't see it that way. For me, in fact, there are three boxes, all separate from each other. I have an idea, and I might put it in the "Don't know' box. I then think about it, and if it makes sense, I put it in the 'Belief' box. I have no evidence that it is true, so it remains in the 'belief' box until there is some evidence to support that belief. When some supporting evidence comes along, I will move it from the 'Belief' box to the 'Know' box.

Later, and increasingly more often, I move it back from the 'Know' box to the 'Belief' box. Now in my advancing years, there is very little left in my 'Know' box.

Criticism and Perfection

I think that how we handle criticism is a major factor in determining our level of happiness, because it goes further than just criticism. It's to do with where we think we are in relation to the rest of the world, what we expect of ourselves, and what we believe others expect of us.

When I was in my early and mid teens, I used to 'beat myself up' with all the 'sins' I committed. I guess this came from my Sunday school education over many years. The sense of not being perfect, not being good enough, not measuring up to what I was 'supposed' to be. It took me a long time to overcome the guilt that parents and society and religion offered me in my formative years, and which I was not sufficiently discerning to reject. The result I think was a repressed attitude to sex, life, love, and the pursuit of happiness.

So I criticised myself, as I had heard the Church 'criticise' the whole of mankind for not being what God – that's their God not the God I now know - would have them be.

I was criticised by my parents, as all children are.

I was criticised at school, as all children are.

I was dumped by the first love of my life, as most teenagers are.

Nobody ever taught us to handle criticism and to have it mean something useful or at least neutral to us. Instead, we are encouraged to feel guilt, embarrassment – 'have you no shame child' - inadequate, irresponsible and all the other negative crap that other people who purport to love us dump on us for all sorts of their own, largely personal reasons.

Is there any wonder we 'lose' teenagers, who, as children were taught to believe that nothing they could do would ever be good enough for the adult world. In fact, after a while, they know that they are not acceptable to society, no matter what they do. To preserve themselves, or that part of themselves and their actions that they define themselves by, they really have little choice but to reject our social world in favour of a peer group who do approve of them, and with whom they can feel valued and significant and worthy.

People learn the most from experience, and when a child experiences a continuous 'don't do that, that's naughty' morning, noon and night, without the corresponding balancing praise for 'good' actions, it's not surprising if they grow up out of the control of their parents and society.

I'm not advocating that we don't restrict what a child does. That would lead to anarchy. But before reprimanding a child, ask yourself 'Why do I want to stop this child's current activity. And the only 3 reasons I can come up with are:

The health and safety of the child and/or others,
Social nuisance and offence,
Damage to property.

Last Sunday I was having a quiet drink in a pub, and a couple came in with their two children – about 5 and 7 at a guess, and they - the kids not the adults - ran riot, screaming and laughing. The parents did nothing to stop them, and the belief that the kids got from that experience can only be that shouting and screaming in a public place is ok.

And for the majority of adults, it isn't. Apart from the nuisance and offence caused at the time, it may well lead to antisocial behavior later.

An explanation by their parents that there is nothing 'wrong' with running about and screaming, just it's not done indoors in a public place, would suffice. After all, I guess those kids have been told that it's unacceptable to urinate in a public place, but never that screaming and shouting is equally unacceptable.

Being continuously and un-heedfully criticised is really not 'useful' to the child or indeed to anyone else.

* * * * * * * *

I remember listening to a piece of music I particularly like. I was getting silently quite emotional about it; the beauty in the

The Self-Help Delusion

harmony, the orchestra, piano and the voice blending in the most brilliant way. Suddenly, my Mother, whom I had forgotten was even in the same room, said "I don't think much of this rubbish, either turn it off, or put on something decent."

The music is nothing until the human brain does something with it to create something in the mind, creating the meaning of the music to the individual listening.

To me it was beautiful, but to my mother, rubbish. Neither is a description of the music, only what two different people were doing with the music.

Criticism is information about how that person is interpreting the event. That is all. You are free to agree or disagree.

That reminds me of a story. Three people go to the ballet. In the foyer on the way out, they were interviewed and asked for their thoughts on the performance. The first, a gruff ex-miner from Barnsley, in quite colourful language said that he thought it was a scandal that public money should subsidise such rubbish. "A load of poufs prancing about in tights, and women built like small barges, swaning around to music." The second, a middle aged businessman, said that, for him it was a new experience, that he had known much of the music for some time, and it was lovely to see it performed in a drama. The third, a lady of advancing years, was clearly moved. She wiped her eyes as she spoke and just said "How wonderful, how completely wonderful".

Of course, none of these comments say anything about the opera, only about how each person is interpreting the opera.

This example provides us with a very important understanding. We can only say the world the way we experience the world. And the way we experience the world is not a description of the world, only a description of the way we process the world.

When someone says something about you that you don't like, that has nothing to do with you.

Someone saying "I don't like that shirt" is an event and the only thing that happened is their saying "I don't like that shirt." - remember the chapter on meaning.

It is not a statement about the shirt. It is a statement about how that person processes the stimulus that they are receiving from their senses when directed towards your shirt, and the way they filter that information and pass it through their history, their beliefs and their prejudices. It says nothing about your shirt.

But how much fun we can have with that sort of comment. Fear, anger, self-righteousness, embarrassment, contempt for the other and a whole mass more feelings, depending on our state of mind at the time and how important that person is to us.

As an example of a different approach to criticism, let's play a conversation. Criticise something about me, and keep on doing it.

Friend: "That shirt's rubbish"

Me: "So I don't think much of yours either." – I'm defending myself.

Friend: "At least it's a decent colour; at least it doesn't look like a Christmas tree." – attacking exaggeration.

Me: "So what makes you the arbiter of fashion all of a sudden?" – defense again.

Friend: "Well, come on, whatever possessed you to buy a shirt that colour." – Personal attack on your sanity.

Me: "Nothing, there's nothing wrong with it." - I'm attempting to justify my choice.

Friend: "Heh, that's your opinion." – Personal attack.

Me: "And what's wrong with my opinion." – More defense.

As you can see, this conversation goes nowhere, and only spirals downwards until one of you gives up, and we are both losers.

Alternatively:

Friend: "That shirts rubbish."

Me: "So what is it about it that you don't like?" – Gather information - with a small smile.

Friend: It's a horrible colour."

Me: "What colour would you prefer me to wear?" – An attempt to gather information.

Friend: "Yellow."

Me: "Right." - An acknowledgement of the information.

And if I know my friend well enough, I couldn't resist - "Don't forget to remind me next time I wear a shirt that you don't like." or, "Thank God. If you'd liked it, I'd have gone home to change".

That approach can add humour, both parties win, the relation-

The Self-Help Delusion

ship stays intact and my friend may not be so quick to criticise my taste next time.

This alternative way to respond to critical comment is very powerful. The realisation that the comment has nothing to do with you, that it is merely information, takes the power out of it and allows for a more light-hearted approach in creating your response.

When you are tired of the artificial drama, change your thoughts about criticism.

Of course, there are times when you can consider the words of another, and examine them in the cool light of reason and decide that there is indeed, some validity in them.

Say you have just started to work for a prestigious company. You turn up for work and your manager says, "That's not a suitable form of dress". OK, then again use the second exchange above, but with a genuinely enquiring attitude to determine what is a suitable alternative dress? After all it matters to you what your manager thinks, and when working for a company you are part of the corporate image that the company has spent years developing. They have rules. If you choose to work for them, abide by the rules. If you don't like the rules, don't work for them. Life is much simpler that way. But it serves you ill to consider the comments as a personal attack on you and your dress sense.

Again, if ten people in the day make the same comment about some aspect of your dress or behavior, and it is something you can change, then seriously consider changing it. If you cannot change it, or you are not prepared to change it, go somewhere where you are appreciated, not criticised.

Some will say that's a cop out and that nothing will ever change if you just walk away. But you now know you have a choice. You can choose to stay and put your efforts into changing the culture and ethos of the organisation. That's a valid choice. You can choose to stay and be a martyr, and get a good feeling from being 'victimised' by the rest of the office. That's cool, though not often very useful to you. It depends on where you are in your life, and if you see that as part of your life's work – even a small part. Ask yourself, 'Is it my job to teach the managers of this company how to make more money and be more efficient', or whatever. If it is, then fine, but always remember, there are none as deaf as those who do not want to hear.

After a critical comment directed at me what I often think, if not usually say is 'Well, if you opinion mattered to me, I could be upset. Since it doesn't...'

The above approach is more difficult to be dispassionate about when the criticisms come from a son or a daughter or a wife. It's not so easy to discount it then.

If it's about something that you can easily change, then it doesn't matter where it comes from, but when it's about your personality, your mannerisms, your beliefs, your arguments, that can hurt.

However, the same approach holds good. Some time ago, I decided to surround myself with people who honor and respect me, i.e., people who do not necessarily agree with me, or hold my views, but who reject them with humour and grace and respect, and the realisation that I did not come by them lightly. I could not be rude or dismissive of those that don't, but I decided to choose not to spend time with them.

Unfortunately, one who dismissed my beliefs with rudeness was my daughter. She is of course totally entitled to her views, but I just chose not to spend any more time with her than I needed to. And that's sad. I love her very much, as a father loves a daughter. I think she's fantastic. But I will not put myself in her line of fire as it were. I love myself too much for that.

And here is the interesting thing. After a particular piece of criticism, I changed my view of the relationship. I realised that she is only another person in the world and there is no reason why her views should matter any more than any other person I know. She is my daughter but she is not my responsibility, and nor are her views. She is a fully fledged adult, and capable of being as she wishes. I used to have the belief that she 'should' be respectful of me because her mother and I raised her, made sacrifices for her as she was growing up, gave her all we could of ourselves.

Then I realised that people will be what people will be, and believing that they 'should' be different because of a past relationship is not a way to happiness. It's a bitter pill to swallow, but the sooner we swallow it, the sooner we will be cured of the suffering

The Self-Help Delusion

we give ourselves because another person is not the way we would like them to be.

* * * * * * * *

Here's an idea about perfection. So often I read from the new age gurus about 'of course you'll never be perfect'. I'd like to look at that assertion. My belief is that I am perfect and I realise that that's a pretty bold statement.

You see, you probably have the same problem with that statement as the rest of mankind has - give or take a few. I really cannot believe that God - if you are into God - made a mistake when he made me, any more than he made a mistake when he made everyone else. I believe that you are exactly as you should be and where you should be at this and every moment of your life.

If you are not perfect in another's eyes, or even in God's eyes, what else should you be? How else should you be? Everything in this world is relative to everything else. And that includes your perfection. If you are not what someone else has a fantasy about how they think you should be, what is that to you?

Other people might think me vain if they heard me say that I am perfect. But I do add that so are you, and so is everyone else. Here of course, people are equating me and my behavior as one. I said earlier, I do not believe I am my behavior. The only criteria I use to judge another's behavior is 'does it work for them in the short term, and as importantly, for them and everyone else in the long term. 'Is my behavior a true reflection of the me that I am striving to be?' is the only question you could usefully be asking yourself. That is the only criteria. Perfection has nothing to do with behavior. Or perhaps more significantly, behavior has nothing to do with perfection.

So I believe that you are perfect, but sometimes your behavior is not representative of who you are, and sometimes it is not useful to you; it doesn't work for you.

I think, if we are not careful, that we are all subject to the fantasy of original sin; that human beings are in some way basically and inherently flawed, like a bowl with a crack in it, and that we have to do something to try and redeem ourselves in the eyes of ourselves and God. Of course this idea has been promulgated by most religions, partly I suspect to maintain power over the people. They say, 'Only we know what you should really be like, as we know what God wants you to be' or words to that effect.

As a side note, one method to maintain control in a relationship is not to be pleased or satisfied. When you let it be known that you are pleased with what the other has done, you become equals and you will loose control. The classic of course is the bitchy woman who never has a good word to say for anyone.

Partners in marriage also do this to maintain the upper hand and to keep their spouse constantly trying to please them. I know of one man who acknowledged to me that it took him 25 years to realise this was the game his wife was unconsciously playing. See appendix for 'Games people Play'.

I think that it is sad that most of mankind has this burden placed on him, not because it is wrong, but because it is not useful to us. It generates fear and guilt, and they are the emotions of anger, self-righteousness superiority – I'm closer to what I should be than you are', and inferiority, 'I know that I have sinned and there is no help in me' To know that you are in some way not what you 'should' be, less than perfect, is not a useful belief.

As you may have gathered, I have no time for the religions of the world that man has maintained faith in for the last 2000 years.

All religion is a story that someone made up some time ago. Each person who helped make up each of the religions of the world had a belief. They created that belief in their hearts, and lived their lives in accord with it. They all claim to be divinely inspired. Maybe they were, and maybe they weren't. I don't know. But just because a belief was formed in someone's mind centuries ago does not make it any more valid than one formed in my mind or your mind today. Each religion tells us what their God wants us to be, and they don't actually vary much in the basics. Once mankind took over the original 'inspired' thoughts, and turned them into hierarchical organisations, then that's where I bow out.

No, we were not born in sin. No, Eve did not cause Adam to eat the fruit of the tree of knowledge. No, God did not make us 'a little lower than the angels'. No, Satan was not an angel who had a disagreement with God. Man, in his quest for control and power created the hierarchies and the conflicts – God v Satan - as though it were a prize fight and we are the prize. We are all equal in the sight of God, and nobody has the divine right to tell us what to believe or what God wants or needs or desires of us. We are each inspired each day to know what is in our interests and in the interests of the greater good. The problem is that we don't listen to ourselves, and we often don't do those things.

Of course, some of the facts in religions are verifiable, but, thinking of meaning, we can only conclude that those who wrote the stories added their meaning to the events. After all, where else can the meaning come from? As we know from earlier, events have no meaning in and of themselves.

Perhaps when you accepted that events have no meaning in and of themselves, you hadn't expected it to have religious significance.

You see, we have this idea that people in the past were in some way 'different' to people today; that they had a direct line to God. That words, thoughts, ideas and actions were somehow received by them, or created in them in a different way than in people today. There is no evidence of this. Mankind was, is and will be, Mankind.

What I am can only be in relation to what another thinks I 'should' be and to what they think their God thinks I should be. That 'should' comes from a fantasy that someone has in his head or a fantasy (one which was assiduously fed to his fertile mind when he was a child) as to what he thinks his particular God has said I should be. I say again, 'We are making it all up.'

Judgment and Opinion

We live in an adversatorial world. Especially in the UK where our government always has a single opposition and the lawyers are not looking for the truth, only to win. It's us and them; right and wrong, good and bad, left and right; 'If you're not part of the solution, you are part of the problem'. 'The friends of my enemy are my enemies'. 'Those who are not for us are against us'.

The media of course flourish on controversy, especially the tabloids. They love a good 'us and them' disagreement. Not for them the middle way of negotiation and understanding, compromise, forgiveness and trust.

Of course not. That doesn't stir the emotions and sell papers. And that is all they are aiming to do. Sell papers, make money, and raise the social prestige of the people involved. The news is just a medium to do that. So we shouldn't be too surprised if they utilise man's greatest enemy (but also his greatest excitement) to do that; fear.

In part because of this, we re-act to differences with the judgmental approach that we have been taught by most of society most of our lives. I'm right, He's wrong.

A friend of mine has recently been on a three day 'Transform Yourself' type course - of which incidentally, I am much in favour. After the first day she rang me and I asked about the day. "His jeans are far too tight for a man of his age" was her first comment. "His sense of humour isn't mine" was her second. Followed by "I didn't agree with… when he said… was wrong… rubbish…" etc.

Now I don't think there is anything wrong in this. It is the way most people think when meeting new people, new ideas, and new behaviors. The problem is that it assists us in noticing and highlighting all those things we don't agree with, and we either miss or reject those things that we could agree with. If we take the time and trouble to attend a course - for whatever reason - we should approach it with an open mind, and expect to have new and different ideas presented to us, and the result of not doing that is that we remain the same person. As I said to my friend, if you believe the same things, and behave the same way after the three days, you'll have wasted your time and your money.

The object of being exposed to new options and behaviors is to have them help you change to a more useful way of processing the world which you are creating, not to reject them because they don't match the criteria that you have formed in your head as to what is acceptable to you and what isn't. And indeed it extends out beyond what is acceptable and believable to you, but also what you think should be acceptable to the world. If only the world would think as I do, then all would be 'right'. But it would be your 'right', not another's right. And that type of thinking is fantasy. People act the way they act, and our not liking it isn't going to change them. Judging them, comparing them or their actions with what you think is good or bad, better or worse is not useful to you in assisting you in achieving what you will for yourself in the world.

People act the way they act from where they are in their mind at the time. The sooner we come to accept another's actions as being the way they are, at that time, choosing to define themselves in this world, the easier life will be for us. Unless we are into drama.

Ideas are the same; if we only ever take our ideas, and reject the view that other ideas present to us, we can never form a fuller and more useful set of beliefs and understandings. And we do not grow.

Think about our eyes. We have been given two, and we use them simultaneously. We don't keep one as a spare to use when the other doesn't work. By using them both at the same time, we create our perception of depth and distance. That's because each eye gives us a different view of the world, and from those two different views, we create a more useful composite view of the world; literally a different view. When we are aware of two different 'views' we can create a third view which incorporates both of the others.

We think we know how other people should behave, how they should speak, how they should look, what they should wear, what

The Self-Help Delusion

they should think. And when they don't do these things, we reject them, or put them in a box labeled 'I don't think so.' and all of their life and experiences, many so different to our own, are lost to us.

I know some people who become very emotional about the way other people dress - the 'Fashion Police' - "Good God, look at that. What on earth does she think she looks like? I don't know, when I was young we used to have to .... ". The media has its fashion police too. Magazines like 'Hello', 'Now', and 'Closer' make their sales and their money telling the rest of the world what it is acceptable to wear and what is not. Which 'look' is in this week / month / season / year and which 'look' isn't. For them, it is a living and a way of life; totally concerned with creating 'acceptable' standards for others to live by. And the others are so concerned what other people think of them that they are prepared to conform to another's fantasy. It's a way to live I suppose.

There is a quotation – "To the degree that you are concerned by what another thinks of you, you are owned by them."

Some people are very scathing of another's accomplishments. "Look at him. Who does he think he is? I remember him when he was a teenager, in court for vandalism and the police were never away from his house, and he got that girl pregnant and then abandoned her – you perhaps don't remember, but I do? Look at him now the puffed up ...."

What do we know how the subject of that ire feels about his past and what do we know about the reason for all that judgement and anger towards him? Nothing. But whilst all attention is being given to the negative aspects of a person, nothing is left over for all the positive ones.

Judgement separates and divides us as human beings. When we separate ourselves from another person, we create a superior and an inferior structure in the relationship. 'I thank God that I am not as other men' to quote the Bible. In our minds, because we believe we are right in our assessment of the world, this automatically puts those who do not think as we do as 'wrong' in their assessment of the world.

Now I am not saying for one moment that I agree with all

the views I hear expressed, or that I wish to dress as others dress, or believe that which others believe. For example, I'm not into the blue pyramid philosophy, where, as I probably imperfectly understand it, you sit under a translucent blue pyramid letting the light shine through onto your head, to assist in achieving a specific mental or spiritual state. At this point in my life, it's not for me. I have no judgement about it. I know nothing about it. How can I reject it as being nonsense, and the people who do believe for being fools, as many do, when I know absolutely nothing about it, either in belief, fact, or experience? The logical part of my nature simply won't allow that.

An open approach to different ideas and beliefs that I have sought out in my life has opened me to beliefs that I now hold which would have been impossible for me to hold ten years ago, even had I been exposed to them then. This book is one outcome of these beliefs.

Someone once said, that in order to negotiate effectively, each party would strive to be able to argue the other parties' case as well as they can themselves. Only then can both parties understand where the other is coming from. How far is that from the arguing, childish 'us and them' attitudes of the petty world we live in? So I'm seeing difference, but not, I hope a judgement of those who see it differently. They have different history and objectives to me, and so of course, they will 'see' things differently. And that's cool.

When people behave in, what to me is a socially unacceptable manner I have to ask myself 'do their actions cause others a problem or are their actions reasonable given the circumstances?' Are there any victims?

It may well be that their action is not illegal; some actions do not do anybody any harm save the person who does the action, and the action may or not be legal. Smoking the drug tobacco is legal, but smoking the drug marijuana is not. Taking the drug alcohol is legal, even though more real crimes involving other people are committed as a result than any of the 'soft' drugs which are illegal. And it's not that people don't not take marijuana etc when it's illegal, they do and in ever increasing numbers; just not openly. I believe we are wasting our time trying to stop people taking soft

The Self-Help Delusion

drugs by making them illegal and telling them that they shouldn't. It didn't work with prohibition in the USA, and it won't work here either. People do not stop doing it because the state says they should stop. As I say elsewhere, my telling you my morality won't change yours.

* * * * * * *

A comment I came across in 'Awareness' by the late Anthony De Mello:

"Anytime you have a negative feeling towards anyone, you're living an illusion.
There is something seriously wrong with you. You're not seeing reality, and something inside of you has to change.
What we generally do when we have a negative feeling is to say, "He is to blame, she is to blame, she's got to change."
No. The world is all right. The one who has to change is you."

What Tony was saying here is that the problem is in your head, not in the other person's behavior. We come back time and again to the totally rational idea that all problems are created in your head. The situation isn't in your head, but your thoughts about it are, and it's your thoughts that make it a problem for you. It's your thoughts you need to change, because you probably cannot change the situation.

Following on from that, I'm now going to make the most fantastic statement in this entire book.

What is, is.

What is, is. That's it. That say's it all. Many of these ideas came from a book by Byron Katie called 'The Work' I urge you to read it. She said:

"When I argue with reality, I loose: but only 100% of the time".

The upshot of this idea is that the world, and everything and everyone in it are exactly what they are supposed to be at this moment in time.

Words like 'should' and 'ought' automatically invoke a judgment. A judgment that says 'I'm right, and the way that it should be is the way I see it' and the way in reality that he or she or it is presenting to me is wrong. That makes a judgment.

Listen to the words you use, because they describe the way you are creating your world. (NLP)

* * * * * * *

Let's look at the words 'Should' and 'Ought'. 'Should' is your own fantasy about how things can be different, in your alternative reality. 'Ought' is someone else's fantasy about how things can be different, and you have taken that fantasy as your own. 'Should' and 'Ought' are words that it is very difficult to manage without in normal conversation. This makes it very important (given what I think you want to achieve) that you know what you mean when you use them.

There are two ways we use the words. The first is in an advisement – see chapter on communication – where someone has outlined a goal, and you might say 'I think you should do xxx' (in order for you to achieve what you have said you want) A more open-choice comment would be 'You could do xxx', which leaves the door open for alternative 'could-s'. This usage of 'should' in this case is positive and directed towards a declared objective, and as such is useful to you and the receiver.

When we say 'You ought to do xxx' (though more usually 'You ought not to do xxx', we are passing on another's ideas - usually from a 'higher' authority - about the way that that authority believes reality (you in this case) should be. It could even be preceded by the authority that it belongs to – 'The good book says that...' The government says that you ought to... 'My Father said that you ought'. It often has a morality or superior tone to it. "You ought not to be doing that you know." from grandmother to her grandson.

The second way we use the word 'should' is when we create our own reality in our head. Very commonly we say things like

The Self-Help Delusion

'he should do that; the world shouldn't be like this; the president shouldn't do this; the prime minister should do that.'

The feelings that accompany the word 'should' when used in this way seem, to my mind anyway to be negative and judgmental. Feelings like indignation and unfairness, failure and regret, anger and irritability, the feeling that something is wrong. 'But it shouldn't be like this.' we protest. 'I recognize that it isn't that way, but it should be. It just should be.' There's a feeling of 'it's wrong that it is the way it is' and so of course that feeling generates a judgement. It's a failure, an admission that the world is not right, and that I am, and that somehow the world has made a mistake. By 'world' here I mean anything or anybody that does or doesn't do whatever it is you think they should, or shouldn't be doing. That may seem a bit OTT. But next time you catch yourself saying 'it ought not to be like this' check what you are feeling.

You see, we create an idea in our head about the way things should be, and when things aren't that way, we get upset about them. It's as though in some way we have been bypassed, discounted, and that my 'common sense' has been ignored when these events were planned and executed. What is happening of course is the realisation that we don't have control of the situation. This event is happening against our will, and there is nothing that we can do about it. And that stores up fear.

As human beings, that part of us that Freud called the ego wants to be able to control everything. And when it can't, it gets afraid because it is the ego's job to order and structure our life. However, sometimes it thinks that another's life is our life, and tries to control and structure that life as well. When it cannot do that, it feels out of control. And being out of control is very disturbing to the ego, and creates fear. That fear turns to anger – all anger comes from fear anyway – and that's where all the negative stuff is generated.

When I hear myself saying 'he should do this' etc, I now ask myself – 'Is this really anything to do with me?' I mean, is it really anything to do with me. When someone says 'he shouldn't do that', the question to ask is, 'what is actually happening?' Is this person doing that, or aren't they? Well, they are. In the real world, they are doing it.

Reality is always right. So, in reality, they should/ought to be doing it, because in reality, they are doing it. Indeed, we are all doing what we should/ought to be doing. We cannot do other than what we 'should/ought' be doing – as there is no 'should' and no 'ought'.

When you are thinking or saying that they shouldn't be doing that, you are flying in the face of reality, because they are. You are opposing reality. All the should-ing and shouldn't-ing in the world is not going to change anything. All that will happen is that you will get angry and frustrated because he / she / it is (or isn't) doing whatever you have fantasised. You have created a fantasy in your mind, and then you have created all these negative feelings when it's not happening like that. You cannot control that reality. We all do this, all the time; and that's nuts..

I use the word 'fantasy' a lot because it conjures up the concept of make believe perhaps better than bland words like 'thought' or 'idea'.

The current emphasis on different sorts of 'rage' – road rage, trolley rage in supermarkets, and no doubt many other examples that the media find catch phrases to describe, these are all examples of a should and shouldn't approach to reality. 'He shouldn't cut me up like that'. 'He ought not to park there'. The meaning that the person creates as a result of these events is not the real reason for the anger. The outburst is an outward expression of an existing inner turmoil. The traffic or the supermarket is just an opportunity to seemingly justify an outward display of anger. The details are irrelevant. Fixing the details does not solve the problem.

* * * * * * *

I remember when a group of us were going home one evening when we were told that the train would be delayed by fifteen minutes. (That's rail speak for thirty minutes.). From then on, a lady in our group spent the entire journey in turmoil of frustration, anger, rolling her eyes, tut tut-ing and in a generally emotional state. The other three of us shrugged our shoulders and got on

The Self-Help Delusion

with the crossword, or passed the time in our usual pleasing and interactive way.

Now I think about it, on another occasion, the same lady, after arriving from London on the evening train said "It ought not to be this cold in April' Now if ever anything 'ought' to be doing what it's doing, it has to be the weather. But even here, that lady had a fantasy about the temperature, and suffered because of it. Not exactly life threatening, but it described perfectly her thought processes at that time

We all do this to some extent. It's part of our thinking process. It's not that its 'wrong', it's just not very useful.

The thing that you 'should' (advisement) be doing in the face of this reality is to ask the question 'what do I do in the reality of this situation?' What can I do? You are the only one whose actions you can control. You certainly cannot control the actions of the world.

'The train shouldn't be late'. The reality is that the train is late. It is useful to accept the reality the train should be late, because the train is late.

If you are saying that it shouldn't be late, that is in opposition to reality. The question that can provoke some useful activity is 'what am I going to do in the face of the reality that the train is late?

* * * * * * * *

This is a very different way to see the world but undoubtedly more 'useful' to you in achieving the contentedness we all seek.

We need to take this reality thing a little bit further. We discussed earlier in the book what is real and what is not. Here we have actions, that either happen or they don't. Their meaning, as we now realise, we create ourselves. The event either has or hasn't happened. Whether you want it to or not has nothing to do with it. And whether you run around saying 'he shouldn't work late, or 'she ought to ring her mother', or not, venting those thoughts is not going to change either the reality or your perception of it. All it does is to create frustration and anger in you. The question is not, how do I get him to stop working late or get her to 'phone her mother? The most useful question is, 'What do I do in the light of the fact that this reality is happening.'

If you process what is happening as, I'm right, and he / she / the Prime Minister / the world - whatever, is wrong, you create a judgement about that event, and once you are into judgement, you are into suffering. Suffering is the difference between the way you see it, and the way you believe it should be. After all, if everything was the way you want it to be, how could you suffer? If you acknowledge and accept that the way it is, is the way it 'should' be because that's the way it is, then suffering disappears.

This is a significant statement. Your suffering is created by the difference between the way you see it and the way it is.

When taken to extremes, this idea may be difficult to support, but the alternative is not very supportable either. For example, if you are dying of cancer and you recognise that at this point in your life, that is the way it should be, and that that's ok, then suffering disappears. Don't get me wrong, the pain doesn't disappear just because of these thoughts, but your acceptance of the pain reduces its power over you. Pain and Suffering are of course, very different experiences (See Chapter on Pain and Suffering.)

* * * * * * * *

Let's now look at the words 'Right' and 'Wrong'. We have a serious hang-up about right and wrong. We seem to have this crazy notion that my right is the right and my wrong is the wrong. It didn't seem that way about reality, so why does it seem that way over right and wrong I wonder?

Over the last few years, my thinking has changed in this regard. It's not that I don't argue over my beliefs of right and wrong anymore. I do, but it no longer matters so much if I am ignored or not believed. It doesn't matter any more. I don't need the rest of the world to agree with me. For me that has been a major change.

The significant thing about the words 'Right' and 'Wrong' is that they are personal judgments, which may not be shared by others. They are sometimes moral judgments, they are not a statement of fact but just a description of the way someone sees the world. And

The Self-Help Delusion

that way is sometimes not shared by those people that we feel the need to share our 'rights' and 'wrongs' with.

'That is wrong' is a statement involving unspoken beliefs, personal values, judgement and morality. And people do not see the world differently as a result of your telling them about your values, judgments and morality. People over whom you have no power certainly don't change their opinion of right and wrong just because you tell them they are wrong.

You will be far more effective if you use the expressions 'useful' and 'not useful' as these express an opinion, but not a judgement. As an example, I believe that taking recreational drugs is not a useful activity and I don't say that as a result of a moral belief or personal judgement. I say it because from the statistics that we have, the evidence points to the conclusion that long term use of recreational drugs makes it more difficult if not impossible to have solid and stable emotional and mental health. Put another way, they fuck you up.

Now. Given that most people do not have being emotionally and physically fragile as one of their goals in life, I would say that taking drugs is not a good idea. There is nothing right or wrong about taking drugs (in my opinion) but it will not help a person live the life that they might 'will' for themselves. Of course it might – self destruction is more rife than one might think, but not a generally held ambition.

Authority is not effective in changing popular culture or behavior because it pontificates about right and wrong, good and bad, and approaches people with a moral line 'we know more than you do and if you do not do as our morality says you should, we will make you a criminal and put you in jail for your behavior which dares to conflict with our morality'.

That way does not work. To verify that statement, look at reality. Is it working? More drug taking, more jail sentences, more crimes committed because of drugs than ever before – in the UK at any rate.

This way does not work. How can I put that another way? **That way does not work**. And doing it harder won't make it work either.

Young people – even people in general - are not interested in someone else's morality and views of right and wrong. But they may be interested in what is likely to help their lives to work and also in what is likely to prevent their lives from working.

Drugs are not a good idea, given the objectives that we believe young people want for their lives. (Not that we have asked them, but that's another story)

Thinking that drugs are 'right' or 'wrong', 'good' or 'bad' is not a useful way to see the situation. Because seeing them that way does not lead to legislative behaviors that reduce the incidence of drug taking.

* * * * * * *

After many years in industry I realised that, depending where you are placed in the organisation, but definitely if you are in middle management, being right in your beliefs and statements is not important. State your case and get out, as it were.

It depending on the ethos of the organisation as to whether or not that approach works. You have to decide before you speak whether what you say will be well received. In some organisations, you will be thanked for caring about the company, and your comments will be noted and perhaps acted upon. In others, you will be accused of negative thinking and blow any chances you might have had for promotion. If the managers of the organisation have their minds fixed on a certain course of action, then nothing you say or do is going to change that. 'Never punch above your weight' was a lesson I learned the hard way.

Being 'right' is not important when their 'right' is not your 'right'. To be a prophet in a land that is not looking for prophets is a thankless exercise. If you choose to challenge their version of right for moral or legal grounds, that's a choice that you are making. Because of that choice, and the ensuing action, there will be consequences. That's fine. But, before you say too much, consider the impact of the possible outcomes on your family and your peace of mind. It may be worth the battle, or it may not. Either way, you sure will learn a lot.

Being 'right' is only important if you are in a quiz game. If your

The Self-Help Delusion

words are valid and in context, then their universal rightness will become evident over time, and if not, you will have saved yourself a certain embarrassment.

And these ideas can be extrapolated to the world in general. In his book 'Awareness', Anthony de Mello has the wonderful expression:

> *"Don't try and teach a pig to sing. It wastes your time, and it irritates the pig."*

If people are not ready to listen, don't try and tell them. You can test the water every year or so, and when they are ready, they will respond and listen. To quote an old eastern saying, "When the Student is ready, the Master will appear."

Right and Wrong are judgments based upon your criteria. They do not exist in reality. Right and Wrong are loose terms. 'Right' when? 'Wrong' says who? We each carry our own right and wrong which we have set as judgments on actions – our own and other peoples, often without knowing the context or the objective of the person who performed the action. And circumstances alter cases. Moral, religious, chronological and social circumstances turn right to wrong and vice-verse.

Burning witches was encouraged by the Christian church, and the torture of non-believers was commonplace. We believe we are 'enlightened' now, and that now we have it about right. But up to the mid 1930's in this country, young women were locked away in lunatic asylums for getting pregnant out of wedlock – the thought being 'For a fifteen year old girl to have sex outside of marriage she must be mentally disturbed'. Or they were 'put away' for the shame they would bring on the family. (See later chapter on Responsibility) And much better to have a daughter who had lost her marbles – poor thing – rather than her virginity. 150 years ago in this country, twelve year olds were hung for murder, ten year old children were put down mines to help make the rich richer, and eight year old girls, and boys too for that matter, were sold to the fat cats of the world for their sexual entertainment.

And they still are being in some countries of the world. The point is that these things were supported, or at least not actively opposed, by the parliament of the day as being 'good', and a socially acceptable way to be behave and the church was certainly not vociferous in its condemnation. But then, for the leaders of the church, the church was far more of a social organisation than a spiritual one. Of course, similar things are happening in other societies, even as you read this book.

Shakespeare, or one of his characters, said "Nothing is either right or wrong but thinking makes it so". I do not say that these things are 'right' or 'wrong'. But there are actions, and there are consequences.

I think any action that adversely affects another's choices should be seriously questioned. To take anything from another person, from their emotional or spiritual or physical well being, seems to me to be inherently wrong, given all the forgoing.

If I use the expressions 'right' and 'wrong' I do not mean them in a moral context, but in the context of effectiveness.

That is to say. If you live in London and you say you want to fly to New York, it is no good getting on a 'plane to Moscow. There is nothing 'wrong' in getting on a plane to Moscow, it just won't get you to New York, which is where you've said you want to go.

Given the laws that govern our society, social crimes like rape and murder are wrong. There, I've said it. They are wrong. But only because those actions are taking us and the victims and perpetrators to Moscow, and not New York, where they and society say we want to go, even if they do not actually realise it.

There is a big difference between what someone might 'will' for themselves, and what they do to attempt to achieve that will. Their 'will' might be good and solid and loving, but the actions they do in order to achieve it might be totally 'wrong'. Put another way, all behavior is only a means to an end, and the end might be laudable, but the behavior may not. Sometimes we set out with the best intentions, but somehow loose sight of the objectives on the way, and end up making the situation far worse. This is why I espouse the idea that 'I am not my behavior'. I am responsible for it but it does not define me – at least at this level.

So the words and expressions like 'should', 'should not' and

The Self-Help Delusion

'ought' and 'ought not' are expressions that are perhaps best removed from your vocabulary if used in this way because they hold a mass of negative and judgmental feelings about the way reality is presenting itself to you compared to the fantasies in your head.

And herein lays the path of suffering.

The Structure of Love

I believe love it to be the most important and misunderstood word in the English language, or any other when translated. It is used as an excuse for a thousand actions, desires, beliefs and relationships, many of which have nothing to do with love as I know the meaning of the word.

As I wrote earlier, words don't have meanings, people have meanings for words. My meaning, definition if you like for the word love is the most useful and the most all encompassing of any I have come across and, for me, clarifies the whole area of behavior around the word and its interpretation.

When I say 'I love you' to someone, I mean "Your will for you is my will for you." What the other person really desires for themselves in their life, I desire for them too. That is all.

To love someone is to make a decision about them and the relationship you chose to have with them. And that's all. It has nothing to do with passion, the rapid beating of the heart, all that romantic stuff. I'll go so far as to say that romance has nothing to do with love.

I believe that love comes about as a decision. You decide, at some level of your mind to love this person.

Love is not an emotion. Love is not a feeling. Love is not most of what romantic fiction would mislead you into believing it is.

Love does not sexually desire another – if there is desire, it's not love doing the desiring. There may be nothing wrong with the desiring, but it's not love that's doing it.

Love does not want or ask anything of another. If there is any wanting something from another, it's not love that is doing the wanting. There may be nothing wrong in the wanting or asking, but it's not love.

Love does not need anything of another. When you need something from someone else, it is not love doing the needing. There may be nothing wrong in the needing, but it's not love.

This resonates with the quality of mercy speech in Shakespeare's 'Merchant of Venice' "It is twice blessed, it blesses he who gives and he who takes" etc. We can think of mercy and love having the same objective – to care about the wellbeing of another. It's the same thing with a different name.

When living together, provided that the relationship is one of equality, and both parties realise what it's all about, then that will enhance a loving relationship. If one party knows that they are taking the other along the road for a different reason to the one they are sharing, then that is deception, not love.

If you want something for someone, but they don't want it themselves, that is not love either. 'But it would be good for you' you might protest. No, it might be good for you in their circumstances, but they are not you, and they are not living your life, and you are not living theirs.

'But he's not right for her, I love her much more than he does'. No. Make your views known, and then show the love you profess by supporting what s/he desires of themselves.

I realise that this is difficult stuff. The greatest love you can give to another is to support them, even when they are planning on doing, or are actually doing something that you believe will not lead them to achieve what they will for themselves.

'What they will for themselves' of course takes a larger view of life than the desires, the wants of the moment. We must be careful that we allow those we love to make choices appropriate to their age and maturity, their knowledge of themselves and the world. With children, we love them sometimes by stopping them doing what they want for themselves, because they may not understand the full implication of what they want at that moment. However, we must also be careful, as they grow up, not to allow our own view of the world to prevent them creating their own.

My daughter, when she was 16, wanted to go to an outdoor 4 day pop concert with her friends. It was in a field somewhere in Essex I think. Do I allow that? What do I know about the risks of

The Self-Help Delusion

modern outdoor pop concerts? Nothing. So I told her that I would like her to go, and I asked questions about what, when, where, with whom, how, etc, to have her think about all the possible situations she might find there. Not tell, notice, but ask, and then I left the decision to her. She went, had a fabulous time and will always remember it as a happy period in her childhood. It might of course have turned out differently. She might have got into drugs or outrageous sex or… anything. I believe my decision was the right one, even though I could have regretted it.

You see, I don't believe there is such a thing as a mistake as we create our lives. Every action is a learning opportunity, even when, or especially when, it does not lead to the desired end. Even if she had 'got into drugs and outrageous sex', that would just have been an experience too. One way we learn is by our own 'mistakes', as well as the 'mistakes' of others. Allow those you love to make their own 'mistakes', and love them anyway. True love is unconditional. That is to say, if you want nothing from another, and you love them, it does not matter what they say, or what they do. That unconditional love will always be there. It's only when you want something from that person that your 'love' can become conditional on them providing what ever it is that you are looking to get from them.

When most people get married, it's as much for what they can get from it rather than the thought of what they can put into it. It is almost impossible to split the wanting to give and the wanting to take, because the wanting to take is from someone who wants to give, and so it is loving to take from them, because that is their will for themselves, to help them define themselves as a giving and loving person.

Part of the problem we have is that 'love' has collected so much baggage that it is smothered in massive emotions for which there are many descriptions, but the description 'love' is not one.

* * * * * * *

Think of another aspect of love, or not, depending how you see it. My mother used to call my sister every morning to get up to go to school. Joan, it's 7:30….Joan, its 8:00…Joan, its 8:15, you'll be late for school

Our mother believed that she was being loving, and helping my sister get to school on time, and in most respects she was. However, forty years later I still heard - Joan, its 7:30….Joan, its 8:00…Joan, its 8:15, you'll be late for work.

I said to my mother. "Mother, how old does Joan have to be before you can believe she will get up on time."

"But she'll be late for work."

"So"

"She'll get told off."

"So. Do you think that she will continue to be late every day if you don't call her?"

Did our Mother love my sister by her actions? Did my sister learn confidence and self sufficiency by my mother's actions? I don't think so. Perhaps it would have been more loving to allow my sister to be late a few times, suffer the consequences, and become more self-sufficient and manage her own timekeeping.

This is not a criticism of my mother. She did the best she could, as do we all, with where she was at the time. She felt she loved her daughter by her actions. She felt needed, and confident that she was doing a good job. And when my sister was a child of 6 she undoubtedly was.

But she didn't change her approach as my sister grew in her ability to tell the time, and look after herself. People expand when they learn to be confident and self sufficient as they grow up, and as a child, their will for themselves is not their immediate need, but to grow into an assured and competent adult is. And it is that will we should have as our will for them.

I had a friend, a work colleague, whom I love. That is to say, her will for her is my will for her. She wants to smoke and has chosen to smoke. I do not smoke, and believe it to be harmful. I know that possible heart and lung disease and an earlier death is not what she truly wills for herself, but it is a behavior she chooses at this moment in her life. That has nothing to do with my loving her or not loving her. I don't nag her to stop, because people do not change just because we might think they should, and nagging

The Self-Help Delusion

her would not be loving her, only salving my conscience about her smoking and seeming not to care. But I do care, and she knows it. But she still chooses to smoke, and I still choose to love her. And I always will.

Here I'm highlighting that, for me there is a difference between what a person might 'will' for themselves, and what they 'want' for themselves.

What they want is not necessarily what they will. Wants tend to be short term behaviors and what a person wills for themselves is more long term, as part of the process of living the life they want in the future, the goals in their life, even if they have never actually thought about it. Sometimes there is a conflict, as with my friend who smokes.

I believe we should support them while they are doing the behavior that they want to do, whilst having their long term will for themselves in mind. Of course we still have to recognise that we have to allow them to make their own choices and live the life they choose to live in spite of our often fervent belief that they are 'wrong'.

* * * * * * *

Taking a more traumatic event; what do you do when someone you love, you wife say, leaves you?

I believe that the same argument applies irrespective of the behavior of the person you love. That is to say, you may not like the actions of another, but you can continue to love the person who does the action, because it is what they have chosen to do at this period in their lives. The only way out of that situation is love. You need to sit back and do nothing. Anything else is a want.

Don't forget of course not to miss out a vital person in all this giving of love. yourself. Loving yourself is also saying 'your will for you is my will for you' – that's you in this case. And you are the most important part of the relationship. Because you must do the things that are representative of the person you are or wish to be, and to love yourself in the same way as you choose to love another.

The question is; who comes first? Do you love yourself more, or the other person?

I believe that you come first. But here is the proviso. You cannot love yourself to the detriment of another – at least without due consideration of the impact on others. For to do so would not be representative of the loving person you choose to be?

It's a catch 22 situation. I say that you should love yourself first, but you cannot give yourself all that you would like because you might know that you want someone at all costs, and that it would not be loving to another to achieve your desire. So you love yourself first, and the other second. But never stop loving the other, and every one around you, and never love yourself to the detriment of another without due consideration of the effect on the other and on yourself. For those decisions define you to yourself in your own heart.

I remember some time ago I had two women friends, and they were friends too. Over lunch with one friend, we were talking about the other, and I remarked how sexually attractive she was, and after a few moments she asked, "Would you go to bed with her if you had the chance"

I stopped and thought about it, and then answered. "No".

"Why not, I though you said that she was very attractive."

"She is", I said, "but I love her too much to go to bed with her, even in the unlikely event that she would want to go to bed with me. I love her too much for that. She is coming up to middle age and looking for a man with whom she can settle down and start a family. I am not that person. Would it be loving her if I were to encourage her into a relationship that could well take up several months if not years out of the relatively short time she has to find a suitable partner, just because I fancy her?"

My friend said, 'would that more people thought like that, there would be a lot less hassle in the world.'

Loving someone does not mean that you have to live with them. Another woman I know has just left her partner of 6 years. As she says, "I still love him, and always will. He's a lovely man, but I don't want to live with him any more." So she put herself first and her partner second. It doesn't mean that she stopped loving him, and it still holds that 'His will for him is her will for him', but to show that love for him to the extent of giving him all he wants, which is for her to continue to live with him, would have been to the detriment of another person whom she also loves – herself. Never love another to the detriment of yourself without due consideration of the effect on the other and on yourself. For those decisions define you to yourself in your own heart.

So you come first – always – but not exclusively.

I think that this puts a different slant on the idea of love. It simplifies it and removes all the emotion and I believe that helps understanding.

We also get tied up with the expressions 'Loving someone' and being 'in Love'.

Creating Relationships
When we first meet another person, we naturally tend to show those facets of our personality that we believe will enable us to get on well with that other person, and we do not emphasis those that we feel would jeopardise the budding relationship. That's only natural because we believe that if we showed all of ourselves, 'warts and all', the other person might reject us right from the word go.

The thing to realise is that other people do the same with us..

When we meet another person, we Delete and Distort and Generalise all that our senses tell us about that person, and we put all those processed experiences into a box, and store that box in our head, and call the box 'Fred Smith' or 'Jane Hillcrest' or whoever.

However, if we continue to interact with that person, we compare and contrast their behavior with the expectations held in the box in our head. Where necessary, we may change the contents of the box in the light of our processed experiences.

But sometimes we have great reluctance to change the mental image of that person even in the light of evidence. The mothers of murderers still see their little boy through rose tinted spectacles.

That's often true, for all sorts of reasons. The way we process the experiences of being with that other person is uniquely ours. How often do we say, when watching friends together, 'I don't know what she sees in him.'

The problems come when we are alone and thinking of the other person and we go to the box in our head called 'Fred Smith' or 'Jane Hillcrest' or whoever, and we play with the memories. In fantasy we add to the contents of the box, and imbue the person with all sorts of attributes that we don't know that they actually posses but we would like them to. We add meaning to what we have already stored away, and create a character in our heads that is not the real person.

You'll probably have noticed that in your conversational fantasies, the other person always responds to you in the way you want them to.

When we 'fall in love' we do this process to perfection, until we cannot tell which is the real person, and which is the person we have created in our heads. And the sensation is wonderful. Nature intended that it be so. It is after all, nature's job to continue the species, and it is not too bothered how it goes about it..

Those early weeks, months, even years in a relationship are the most exciting experience there is. Both parties have the perfect person, because both parties have enough sensory experience added to what they have created in the box in their heads to be with the only person for them in the entire world. We respond to the other person as best we can because we want to please them and to be for them what they are for us, and vice-verse. And we stretch our behavior to be what we believe the other requires of us.

After a while, we start to ask things of the other person. And the real personality begins to become apparent to us but again we suppress that evidence and we continue to act out of character and to believe the other person really is the person we believe them to be.

Finally, the charade cannot continue any longer, and we realise that the person we fell in love with has changed so much, and is not the person they were when we first met them. They are of course, we just didn't create them in our head the way they were, or have become in trying to be what they think they have to be in order to be in the relationship. 'Love is blind' as the poets have been telling us for centuries.

We fall out of love because as it were, 'the scales are lifted from our eyes', and we 'see' the person as they really are – to us anyway, and we believe that we have been fooled, and deceived, and let down, and we are angry with the other person for the sudden change in their character.

But we did most of he deception ourselves. People fall out of love because they created a lot of the other person in their imagination, and that person does not exist in reality.

Finding Love
Some time ago, when my life was not a bowl of cherries, and I was generally feeling sorry for myself. You know, Billy-no-mates, no friends, still searching for love in my life, even though I'd been married at that point for over 20 years, and generally not liking myself much, and I couldn't see why anyone else could like me, let alone love me. I really was an old misery guts, close to a nervous breakdown, and heading for depression.

Then I came across the philosophy and technique of communication known as NLP – Neuro-Linguistic-Programming, that suggests that we ask ourselves questions, one of which is 'How do I know what I know, and if it's about something I want / need, how will I know when I have it?' It teaches to look more carefully at what we know, and determine if that knowledge is well founded in reality, and not just created in our own heads.

Anyway, whilst studying NLP, I was prompted to ask myself the question 'What would someone have to do, for me to know that they loved me?'

I came up with the following:

They would have show they respected me by listening to me – though not necessarily agreeing with me.

They would have to show that they supported me by arguing my case with others – even if they didn't totally agree with it themselves.

They would have to show that they liked me by being prepared to spend some time with me – when they didn't have to.

They would have to show that they cared for me by thoughtful actions.

They would have to show tolerance of my shortcomings by not being critical of my errors and failings.

They would have to be accepting of me in all I think, say and do, though constructively pointing out where they feel I might be mistaken.

Then I looked at the relationships I had with several people and a minor miracle happened. I suddenly realised that many people loved me, and that in consequence I must be a loveable person. It all seems so obvious now but at the time it was an awakening. I had been so constrained by my belief that I had in some way to 'find' love and, because of this belief, I couldn't recognise love even if I did have it. I thought we have to look for love, to find it somewhere like one might find a particular CD or a lost cat. I didn't know where to look, or how to recognise it if I found it. It had never occurred to me to look inside, not outside. I already had love. That one question did it for me. 'What would someone have to do for me to know that they love me?'

Many people bewail the 'fact' that they don't have love when what they often mean is that they don't have anyone to 'sleep' with. And of course, because many people don't realise the difference, they don't realise that there are people in their life who do love them. Even if it is only their probation officer.

Then I had to ask myself, why do these people, my friends, love me? How come some people seem to find so many 'bad' people to accompany them through parts of their life, and others seem to find 'good' people. I had so many 'good' people in my life, and very few, if any, 'bad' people. Maybe I should define 'good' and 'bad'. 'Good' people are those who are supportive, thoughtful, concerned, helpful, and positive and accepting of me and 'bad' people are those who aren't.

Of course when you look at the attributes of good people, they are the same attributes as those who love you.

So why are they loving to me? They have other people in their lives that they don't display these loving attributes to, so why do they display them to me?

And then the second great truth struck me. Perhaps they love

The Self-Help Delusion

me because I love them. So if I am loving, then people will love me? And if I am not, people won't?

And the answer to that one is 'Yes'. That is the way it works the best. Not always, and there are exceptions to every rule. But on average, and generally, you get back what you give out. To quote the bible, "It is more blessed to give than to receive." I heard that when I was 5 years old, and didn't believe it until I was 50. At least, I didn't understand it, and it didn't seem to make any sense. How, by giving away something, could you gain more of it?

Do you remember earlier, when I spoke about you creating your own reality? Think of the process of creating your life as like baking cakes. You bake your world-cake as you 'see' it in your own head. And when you make your world-cake with love, that's the way the cake comes out. Your life consists of the ingredients you put into it. It is that simple.

* * * * * * * *

We can extend these ideas into the workplace. We often meet more people at work and have longer conversations with people at work than with most people in our private lives – even our spouse - and that's one reason why so many personal relationships begin at work.

Another and I believe the major reason why that is true is that we require nothing from our work colleagues to support our way of life, our expectations or our responsibilities. They don't look after the kids when you need (want) some time off. They don't pay the mortgage, or take the garbage out, or vacuum the lounge or... anything. There are no obligations either way between you. There are no personal needs, and no personal wants outside of the relationship. And that can make another person seem very attractive.

And indeed be very attractive. No needs, no ties, no children, no responsibilities, no unspoken bargaining. It's easy to say 'I love you unconditionally' because all the circumstances that create conditional love are not present in that relationship.

Given the foregoing to be valid, conditional love is a figment of our imagination. Conditional love says "I'll love him until he does something unacceptable to me, and then I won't love him". So then he has to satisfy some desire or need I have for him to be or do what I want him to be or do, or at least not be what I don't want him to be or do. At that point, my love depends on his doing and being and saying what I want him to do, be or say, and if he doesn't then I won't love him. Well I mean, he won't be deserving of my love if he does … will he?

'Need' and 'want' can be the death of love. Domestically we generally 'love' on condition that spoken or unspoken tasks are performed, expectations met, obligations undertaken. We use our partner to satisfy our domestic requirements, for physical comfort, for sex or to do little jobs for us, to make life easier for us. We use our partner to make life easier for ourselves. And then and only then do we tell them we 'love' them, and we are prepared to accept their 'love'.

That is not love as I define it. That's a trading arrangement. I'll trade you what you want if you'll trade me what I want. And we'll call it love. But it isn't. And when our partner fails to do all the things that we require of them, we don't feel 'love' for them. And if we have mistakenly attached love to desire, and we are taught to do that by the misuse of the word 'love', then we don't desire them any more either. Conditional love generates conditional desire. And that's death to a marriage.

We get into an 'I don't see why it should be me that always has to…' kind of relationship, and the other party isn't playing the game the way you want it played.

Most don't realise what the rules are, nobody told them before they vowed to 'love, honour and obey' They thought that you would love them irrespective of what they did, and now they are realising that there's a price to be paid for that 'love' and the price wasn't on the menu when the matrimonial lunch was ordered and delivered. The appetizers lasted for a couple of years perhaps and they were great, but when it's time for the main course, usually taking between 20 and 40 years, the rules suddenly change, and one party becomes a convenience and the trading begins. "I don't feel like it tonight, you can't expect me to switch on when you aren't 'loving' during the day."

The Self-Help Delusion

Someone once said that sex is only 40% of marriage. Problem is, it's the first 40%. Of course, that leaves 60% of the relationship to be managed harmoniously. If the wants and needs of each party are not satisfied in the 60%, that then that disappointment leaches into the 40% and the marriage fails. The protagonists may not separate, but it won't be a happy marriage.

That's the way most marriages work. Or don't work. And from the divorce rates, most don't work after the first few years, and the lives of most of the combatants who stay together become lives of quiet desperation.

Like I said, need and want are the death of love.

So many people make their marriage into a battle ground, trying to keep one up over their partner, to use and manipulate them to get what they want. To bargain and trade favours. It may work. But there is no openness, no deep joy, no sharing of the heart in the small hours of the morning, because each is maneuvering the relationship for their own ends, each trying to get from, rather than to give to the other. And the reason they do that is because they do not believe their partner has unconditional love for them. They believe they have to be what they think their partner signed up to when they decided to become partners, that they would not be keeping their part of the bargain which passes for love in that relationship.

A friend of mine made a disclosure to me on one occasion. I can't remember the details, but nothing major. "Have you told your partner this," I asked. "Good God no, he'd never understand".

She could tell me because I'd previously told her that I loved her unconditionally. But she couldn't tell her partner, because they have a trading arrangement, and she believes his love is based on her being the sort of woman he wants, not on what she actually is or wants to be. And that could be because that is the way she 'loves' him too. And that's sad.

A few years ago, I was lucky enough to be working with many graduate young people, and I found them enchanting. I loved their enthusiasm, their drive, their courage, their honesty, and the love they showed their colleagues.

There was one young woman that I seemed to have a special

connection with. Maybe it's my feminine side coming out to play at last. Maybe in the soul life we had agreed to recognise each other in this one. I don't know. Anyway, we were on the balcony of a nearby pub, looking out over the water. We began talking seriously, and I gave her my definition of love – your will for you is my will for you – and I just had the urge to say, "and I love you. I want nothing from you, I just love you." She said "Unconditionally?" and I said "Yes. Unconditionally. I want nothing from you, and it doesn't matter what you do, or if you never speak to me again, I'll always love you." We hugged each other and kissed cheeks and she went in to the pub to join her boyfriend. And I know that she loves me too even if she cannot say it, because deep down, she does not have my definition for the word love.

I still see her every now and again. I met her fiancée whom she subsequently married, now with two children, and I'm happy that her will for her is working out just as she wants.

Now I don't know what that experience did for her, but I know that I learned a lesson from that evening that changed me forever. I think that was the first time that I said 'I love you' to one of my colleagues. By voicing the unconditional love I have for her, I made it real in our lives, and I knew from then on that I have love to give away, and I found out by experience that I am a loving person, and being a loving person is now one of the ways I define myself to myself and to the world. I gave love away only to get it back. I did not tell her I love her so that I could hear her say it back to me. In fact she didn't. When I gave her my love – if only a statement of love, I realised that I had love to give away. And if I have love to give away, then I must have love, because you cannot give away that which you do not have.

And for the first time in my life, I realised that 'it (really) is more blessed to give than to receive'. It's not just a trite expression from the Bible. It actually works. It describes the way the human mind operates. Only when you give something away do you actually realise (make real) that you have it. So I have love in me to give away. That was a major 'wow' experience.

Love and Sex

Where do I start on this one? There is nothing to say that has not already been said in one place or another. However, think about what we said previously about meaning. Nothing has meaning but the meaning you give it. This implies that the sex act of itself has no meaning. No more meaning than anything else has. We give it whatever meaning we choose.

Most people think that it must mean what they think it means, and anyone who doesn't see it as they do is wrong; in some cases morally degenerate.

Lots of people will tell you what sex 'really' means, just as there are lots of people who will tell you what everything else 'really' means:

Three examples:

The Christian Church says - The coming together of two people, in truth and honesty, to experience the most intimate act that human beings are capable of. It's a sacred act, only to be experienced within the sanctity of marriage, a holy act, ordained by God for the procreation of children to the greater glory of heaven; or words to that effect.

The Lover might say - She is just so beautiful, and my heart just melts when I see her asleep, and I just want to be part of her, and make love to her and make her happy.
The porn star might think - I enjoy sex, and being paid to do it is fantastic.

The clubber might say - A quick suck and shag in a doorway on the way home, with someone I've never seen before, and wouldn't even want to if I were half way sober. Just so long as I get my rocks off.

The Rapist thinks - F*****g women. They just ask for it, the c***s, they deserve all they get.

They have each created their meaning, and of course, there are as many meanings as people. I've just illustrated the point with examples. You have to decide what a sexual experience means for you.

Unfortunately we are led by society and the media and by human nature to believe that sex is love and love is sex.

When we get married, we naturally vow to be faithful to that one person. Though these days, vows tend to have far less religious significance. Few really believe we are dammed to eternal hell if we break the strictures of religion. And people do break them, sometimes with impunity. And as always, there are consequences.

When one partner commits adultery, and because that act has no meaning either, we have very varied responses from the faithful partner as they create their own meaning. Very few can forgive and forget. The relationship will never be the same again. Often the most painful aspect is the deception and the dishonesty of the partner, and the actual sex act - particularly if it is the man who has strayed - is more easily forgiven. When trust has been broken, it cannot be created again as it was the first time. The response of the injured party depends entirely on the meaning they have given to sex and marriage in their belief system. If they believe that the spouse still loves them, and only wanted a little spice in their life and that they will always come back to them, then they could just turn a blind eye and perhaps the marriage will remain stable.

I think that some people without a definite partner have sex with someone they hardly know, in the hope that they might feel loved, and persuade themselves that the other person does love and care for them. But after a while they realise they don't really.

Some people go looking for a one night stand with no thought whatsoever for the other person who at that point is only another body to use. Just to take from them. Or to give no more than they have to in order to take what they want. People have taken from them in the past, and there is no way they are going to get emotionally involved and be hurt again. So they put on the trading approach. I'll do this for you if you'll do that for me. And to some extent that works.

Other times of course, both parties simply want uncompli-

The Self-Help Delusion

cated sex, and nobody is obviously hurt. They may however love themselves a little less as a result.

It is all a learning and growing process. And if you can come out of the process with your emotions unscathed, or at least, not scattered so far a field as to make them irrecoverable, then you can consider yourself lucky; because many people don't. We know when we have been cheated and betrayed, and we tighten up our defenses, and batten down the hatches of the heart. And with an attitude of "I don't give a damn", the heart appears to be safe and secure, and it is – for a while.

It reminds me of a story from the deep south of the USA

A red necked Texan was talking to a friend about the ******* blacks in his town. "I'm totally against the blacks integrating the way they want. If I had my way, I'd put the whole damned lot of them in a big barrel and sit on it. That would teach them; they'd be going nowhere."

His friend said "That's true Elmo but unfortunately, since you are sitting on it, neither would you."

Locking up the heart is fine if you want to live in a cocoon, in an emotional vacuum, not experiencing all that you are capable of. And of course it's very safe. But it's ultimately unfulfilling, because you are spending all your energies protecting yourself, and not opening to the possibilities that other people offer. If you take everything personally as perhaps you used to, then loving someone was very painful if they decide that you were no longer the apple of their eye or flavour of the month as it were.

But now your love for them says – "Your will for you is my will for you", and you let them go to live their lives the way they chose.

You might think that you couldn't just walk away. But ultimately you have no choice. That other person does not choose to be with you, and all the 'love' in the world will not change their mind. You are not what they want at this point in their life.

Most people cannot just walk away. Most people kick and fight and plead, and threaten and beg and then have to walk away. Because there is no choice; you cannot give another person the personality that you would like them to have so that you will be what they want. The question is not, do you walk away or not, the question is how much kicking and fighting and pleading and threatening and begging are you going to do before you do walk away. All the expectations you had for your future life may have just been blown apart. Nevertheless, the only way to create peace of mind is to realise that if you really 'love' that person as you have said you do, then you can only let them go with your blessing. Otherwise the 'love' you profess you have for them is actually your need, want and desire for your life to be made easier within that relationship. Your love is actually a desire, want and need, not an unconditional 'your will for you is my will for you' love at all.

A fiend of mine once said "I don't make love every time I have sex, but I would never have sex with anyone I didn't love."

Of course, you have already decided for yourself what your take is on this. That decision is still open. In the really important aspects of life, there is no such thing as a decision, fixed and final. We are not a fixed entity; we are all a work in progress.

Love is about openness, and trust, and freedom and giving and forgiving and opportunity. Anything which constrains those things is not love. When you seek to take from another or not give to another that which you can unless it takes from you, then that is not love. When you seek to constrain another because they seek to change their life against your wants or desires, then that is not love. When you seek to hold another by emotional force or blackmail, then that is not love. And sex can be used to do all of these things.

Desire and Love are not the same thing

Desire is: See it, want it, take it.

Love is: See it, it wants, give it.

And of course, when you 'fall in love' there is a conflict between these two opposing attitudes. And it's the internal conflict that makes it so irresistible

Love and Friendship

It seems to me that love can be a one-way process, and friendship is a two way process.

I believe that friendship is conditional on what the other person does or does not do, whereas love is unconditional, and will be there irrespective of the other's actions.

The Self-Help Delusion

This means that, since all people can be encompassed by unconditional love you can love someone, but they may not be your friend. I love my wife, but she is not my friend. She does not give me those things I need from a friend. But I still love her.

I made the decision to love her a long time ago. That has not changed, nor ever will. We are not friends as we do not behave to each other in the ways we need to consider our spouse as a friend.

There's a lot of water passed under our mutual bridge during the last forty five years of marriage, and we have both become quite different people. I guess we have both become disappointed in each other, one way or another. We are each not as the other saw us for the first few years, and the magic of our youth has passed. We have not grown together, but apart.

We choose to spend time with our true friends, and they with us, as a symbiotic relationship where both parties gain. If you are in a one way friendship, an out of balance relationship, it may well not useful to you over a long period of time.

Some friendships are therapeutic, where one party acts as a mentor, and both parties have their needs met. One person can have the joy of passing on understanding or wisdom, and the other person to have the undivided attention of another with the intention of learning and growing and changing their world.

You may have known friendships that were far from therapeutic, where one party did all the taking, and the other all the giving. However, perhaps that was where each party needed to be at that stage in their life. Eventually, one or the other would realise that the dynamic of the relationship was caustic to them, and move away. That's difficult to do, as for each, at that stage in their life, the relationship served them. And then one party decided that it doesn't anymore. Both parties would be wiser after the event, and perhaps be aware when such a relationship was occurring again, and change the dynamic.

I remember the quotation 'No two people ever come together for the benefit of only one'

In one twenty year long relationship, I was acting as friend, coach and mentor. At one point I said that I would be happiest when our relationship changed, and she didn't want me around anymore. She was upset and said that she would always want my friendship. I didn't argue but about two years later, she said 'I'm sorry that I haven't had time for you recently, but I've been so busy doing my own thing, I just didn't need you around."

"Good", I said.

I still see her, but not often. She doesn't need my friendship anymore. My job is done. I still love her, and she knows that, but she doesn't need me anymore. Our relationship ran out of purpose, for her and for me.

An Analysis of Responsibility

To define 'Responsibility' the dictionary uses expressions like 'Morally accountable', 'Answerable to another for..', 'Obligation', 'Charge', 'Trust', 'Duty', 'capable of fulfilling an obligation'.

So I'll ask the obvious question. What do you think you are responsible for in this life?

Let's think of it like this. In business, one of the really nasty binds you can be placed in is when you have responsibility without authority or knowledge; to be responsible for some activity, or event or somebody else's actions, without the power to control or direct them. This is very likely to cause you tension and stress, especially if the consequences of the failure to control or direct has a significant bearing upon you in one way or another – promotion chances, salary, redundancy etc. Of course the situation is not useful to the organisation either. Your manager or those above him/her believe that things will run smoothly because, after all, the responsibility has been assigned and there should be no problems. Unbeknownst to them they have set-up both you and the events for failure, because they have not given you the power to affect the situation in any effective way. Not good.

Transferring this idea to your partner and friends? Where do your responsibilities lie there? And my answer to that is – nowhere. Some would say that I'm opting out, but there are two reasons why I say this. Since you have no valid control over them, you cannot change their thoughts and actions. And since by now I hope you are beginning to believe that you alone are responsible for your thoughts and actions, it follows that others must also be responsible for theirs.

In other words, they will do as they choose. Rationally, how can you be responsible for the beliefs and actions of another, when you have no control over them?

We often take on impossible responsibilities. How can we consider ourselves responsible for the activities of say a 25 year old son on drugs, or a 30 year old daughter who wants to divorce her (to you) perfectly acceptable husband? That's silly. They are fully fledged human beings, creating and living their lives the way they choose to.

As I see it, I am responsible for:

1. My actions and their foreseeable consequences,
2. My emotions and my subsequent behaviors,
3. The preservation of my physical and emotional health,
4. The preservation of the physical and emotional health of others where reasonable,
5. The preservation of my wealth and the wealth of others,
6. The honoring of another's decisions and beliefs except where they violate 1 to 5 above,

The first three are about your responsibilities to yourself, and the last three are your responsibilities to others.

Taking the first three; I am responsible for my actions, my emotions and my subsequent behaviors and the preservation of my physical and emotional health and foreseeable consequences.

Often other people, usually partners, subtly move the responsibility for their happiness on to the other. If only he would do this, or if only she would do that, I could be happy. Since there is no way I can change another's view and attitude towards themselves and the world, I cannot reasonably be responsible for their state of mind. The responsibility to make you happy is yours, not mine. And the responsibility to make me happy is mine, not yours.

People often say, 'He makes me so happy', under the belief that their happiness is as a result of their relationship with another. And at that point it is as a result of their relationship. And they say it like that because that is the way they think about it. That really translates to "I can allow myself to be happy when we are together", along with the unconscious thought that 'I cannot allow myself to be happy when we are not together', coupled with 'and it's his/her fault if I'm not happy.' This is not a useful belief as we can neither control their behavior nor their 'love' for you.

Put another way, you are giving the control of your happiness to another over whom you have no control. You alone are responsible for you; your beliefs, your thoughts, your actions and your physical wellbeing. You are not responsible for how another person chooses to live their life. You are creating yourself and your life as you choose it to be - whether you know it or not - and so are they.

Man has a great desire to tell others what to believe, what to think, what to make real and what meaning to place on events, what to eat and what not to eat, who to love and who to hate, what to feel guilty about, what to feel ashamed about - and everything else in between.

* * * * * * * *

Taking the last three;
'The preservation of the physical and emotional health of others where reasonable'

From this I can make the statement, I have no responsibility for my grown-up daughter. I may choose to assist her as and when I can, but that is a choice I am entitled to make, not an obligation imposed on me by the relationship.

I decide what is reasonable. If the problem is one I can fix without any undue losses to myself, than I will fix it. Only I can decide what 'any undue losses' might be.

It seems to me that "Half the 'problems' in the world are created because half the people in the world want to live other people's lives for them." For problems read misery, unhappiness, frustration, anger, bitterness, abuse, murder and war. Yes, even war. Many wars are fought over ideologies – you will believe what I believe or I will kill you until you do. Extremists of various ideological persuasions see it as their responsibility to convert the world to their way of thinking because they are 'right', and all others are 'wrong'.

I've finally realised that the only universal truth is that there is no universal truth.

In some cultures, the parents still consider themselves to be responsible for their adult children, especially daughters, even as to who they will marry and when. Recently I read of a murder case where a father found his adult daughter in her bedroom with her boyfriend. The boyfriend ran, and the father went to get a knife, came back, and murdered his daughter by stabbing her 20 odd times. He was nuts you might say, but what beliefs did he need to hold to do that? Where the belief that his daughter's behavior was so wrong, and the shame it brought on himself and his family was so great, that he felt he needed to murder her to assuage the wrongdoing. What a terrified man. An extreme case, but it illustrates the point.

There are many cases of just such ideas giving rise to women being murdered for marrying someone they love rather than accepting the arranged marriage that their parents want for her. One has to wonder that if the family 'loved' their daughter, how come they want to kill her. Pride and honour and tradition are hard taskmasters.

When you were young, and even slightly involved with the Christian church, you will have been told to believe "I am my brother's keeper." This is a very dangerous belief. It's easy to interpret that expression so that taking on the responsibility of the lives of others may give you a warm feeling as a solid person, caring about others, standing up for what you believe to be right, and excluding from your life all those things you have decided are wrong. That's fine – for you. But others should be allowed the same freedom. Live your life as you see fit, and let other's live theirs in their way, by their standards. They have nothing to do with you. You are not a reflection of another's behavior, good or bad, and their behavior is not a reflection of you. In some societies, family honour is more important than the happiness of individual members, as in the case above. It's a sort of communist style family, where the value of an action is judged first and foremost by how well is supports the family and it's position in the community, where the family is greater than the sum of it's parts; where the actions of one member of the family reflects badly on another, and brings shame on the whole family and all the members of that family. Members of an extended family are often shunned when a brother or a son commits an unacceptable

The Self-Help Delusion

act; divorce, adultery, marriage below their status, embezzlement or whatever.

The people who accept all this vicarious responsibility have their lives permanently damaged / changed as a result, as do the people who have their lives taken away from them by well meaning members of the family.

All this is neither good nor bad, but there is a price to be paid. To every action there is a consequence, and each person involved creates a meaning, and because of that meaning, they change – their beliefs, attitudes, responses, actions.

I say again. You are responsible only for you; only your own beliefs, thoughts and actions, not someone else's. I am not responsible for how another chooses to live their life. You are creating yourself and your life as you choose it to be. So are they. This is what I believe.

You may have a problem with that idea. Ask yourself, 'who is responsible for my life and how I live it'? Then ask 'who is responsible for another's life and how they live it'?

Note that I'm not saying I'm right, and others are wrong, all that I am doing is to suggest to you, other things to believe, other ways of thinking and other possible responses to events. That's all. If you aim to make them true in your life, that's cool. And if you choose not to, that's cool too.

All the foregoing does not seem to leave much space for love, or helping others; easily interpreted as look after number one, and sod the rest.

But notice what I am saying, not what I am not saying.

I am not saying that when the other person is young, or some way unable to make a considered judgment for themselves, and you are in a position of responsibility in regard to them, that you should accept that responsibility to a degree in keeping with their dependency upon you, to attempt to control their actions as far as you are able. The 'child' can be any age but in western society, around 12-14 is perhaps the point where they have some appreciation of the 'real' world and their own views begin to take precedence over yours.

I am not saying that you shouldn't care, that you shouldn't help, that you shouldn't advise, that you shouldn't listen and question. If they are your friends or family, then you love them, and love says, "Your will for you is my will for you." Help to ensure that the other person is aware of the possible consequences of their actions, and then stand back to allow them to create themselves and their lives in the way that they choose. That is love as we spoke of earlier.

I am not saying that any form of behavior should be tolerated. Those who seek to interfere in the lives of others by aggressive behavior, physical or verbal, need to be either handled or avoided or in extreme cases, removed from society and where possible, educated until they no longer have that tendency. Unfortunately, sometimes it's a whole country that interferes, or a fundamentalist religion or a dictatorship, and they are not so easy to ignore.

Those people who are ignoring the numbers 4 - 6 in the list of human responsibilities are a challenge to us and the kind of life we wish to lead, and there are such 'toxic' people around. Avoid them like the plague until you are strong enough in your self-worth to remain unaffected by their ignorance. That doesn't make you better than them, but perhaps just more aware of what negative behavior does to them and to others. They are the challenges in your life. If you continually fail to rise to the challenge that any specific person offers you, move out of their world and spend time with another who offers smaller challenges until you have created your strengths both in your beliefs and your approach to such abuse. You will then be in a good emotional position to spend time with challenging people and use their attitudes and beliefs to discover hidden depths within yourself, and who knows, even help them realise that yours is not a better way, just a different way, and that by example show that happiness flows more readily from your approach to life than it does from theirs.

If they don't see it, that's alright. Don't forget of course, that if we want to be different, we have to change. Change our beliefs and behaviors, and give up the emotional involvements that fill so much of our lives. Drop the Drama.

There's a quote "Other people are not here this time around to fulfill your fantasy about what you think they ought to be".

Looking at Trust

Let's take a brief look at the concept of Trust.

For me, trust is a faith or belief in something or someone; that the train will be on time, that the milkman will call, that my partner loves me. I would call that an external trust, in happenings outside of you. As with communication, there are two directions for trust. There is the trust we have for something of somebody outside of ourselves, and the trust we place in our own selves.

Internal Trust

This is the trust you have in yourself not to let yourself down, not to do anything you will later regret, to uphold your highest values, to confirm by your actions, the you that you have defined yourself as being.

Sometimes we don't live up to this ideal, and what we do afterwards is very important.

It's very easy to beat up on yourself, to criticise yourself, and generally feel bad about it. I think it more useful to forgive yourself. NLP has the belief, 'everybody does the best they can from where they are in their awareness at the time'. This includes you. You did the best you could from where you were in your awareness at the time.

Instead of listening to all the negative crap that you tell yourself after such an event, ask yourself questions like - where was I in my mind at the time? What influenced me to behave like that – (remember, 'I am not my behavior') why did I do and say what I did? How can I behave differently next time that situation arises? Cut yourself some slack. Spend a little time in regret, and a lot of time picking the lesson from the event.

That is the only useful way to process the event.

External Trust
Most people think about trust in respect of their relationships with other people rather than their relationship with themselves. How can we learn to trust other people? Indeed, is it wise to trust other people? I have been let down so many times by people who I thought I could trust.

When we meet another person, we naturally tend to show those facets of our personality that we believe will enable us to get on well with that other person, and we do not emphasis those aspects of ourselves that we feel would jeopardise the budding relationship. We looked at these ideas in the chapter on Love.

It's a pity, but true nevertheless. We each behave the way we think we need to behave in order to be attractive to the other person whose company we seek. The thing to realise is that other people do the same with us. And after a time, we say things like: "I thought I knew him." And "How could she do that to me."

We feel that they have let us down when in fact they were only showing another aspect of their personality that up to now, generally unconsciously, they had kept hidden. When they allowed it to come to light, they did not do so as – 'I know, I'll let that person down now'. They just did what they would naturally do. They felt safe in the relationship and they relaxed a bit and just became more of themselves. They did not let 'you' down. They would have done it with anybody. They did not single you out. In fact, they probably did not even think about what they were doing. Most of this activity is driven by the unconscious mind anyway.

The bottom line is that we did not know that person as well as we thought we did, and we filled in the rest in our heads. Just like when we fall in love, we assumed that that person had the qualities that we imbued them with. And they didn't.

Was that their fault? Are they to blame because they were not as we had thought them to be? Their communication was flawed, in that they transmitted what they thought we wanted, but in fact we have given it a different meaning.

A long time ago, I had an evening meal with a friend. It was a general disclosure session, and she told me lots of things about herself that I guess she doesn't tell many. She realises that her

The Self-Help Delusion

past actions would not be acceptable to many others because she believed their love to be conditional. She knew I loved her unconditionally, and hence she was prepared to say all she did.

"Now I've told you all that, what does that make me?" she said.

"That doesn't make you anything" I said. "You are no different to me now than before you told me. You are not your behavior, and I made the decision a long time ago that your will for you is my will for you'.

If she had told those things to a prospective boyfriend on the first date, I suspect that may well have run a mile.

People disclose what they consider are the adverse or unattractive things about themselves after they have shown the more attractive sides of their personality. And of course, what they consider as unattractive to others are also the things that are unattractive to themselves. Those actions are not true to the person they desire to be. They may have forgiven themselves, but the regret is still there. Only by eliciting the acceptance of others can most people begin to truly accept themselves.

So I'm saying that those things about you that you are reluctant to tell to others are those parts of yourself that are not truly you. It is you of course, but you have not come to terms with that part of you yet. By telling someone you trust – someone who loves you unconditionally – about that part of your history or behavior, you can begin to accept and embrace that part of you and become whole again.

Unfortunately, not many people have someone whom they believe loves them unconditionally. And that is because they do not love themselves unconditionally. Remember that you cannot give away that which you do not have, and that is another reason why it is more blessed to give than to receive.

Just because you love someone unconditionally, it does not mean that they love you. Nor does it mean that they have good intentions towards you. Some people we love tell lies in order to deceive us and in some way take from us or to use us for their own ends. It might simply be money, or maybe our secrets, or our body, or our reputation or any one of a dozen things which we feel we need to be ourselves.

We create events in our life, and the meaning we give them will be all our own. A woman under the belief that the man 'loves' her may well welcome intimacies that she wouldn't otherwise. Of course he may not love her, he maybe thinks that he loves himself and is out for all he can get for himself. As long as she provides it, he is quite happy. After a while, he moves on to something else he fancies he 'loves'. For her, this can be a devastating negative experience such that she says to herself 'I will never trust a man again' and as a result, her behavior becomes more like that of the very man she despises. Quite understandably, she begins a relationship to take from it rather than to give to it.

I was 'chucked' when I was about 20, and I remember my motto at the time, 'Get what you can while it's going, because it may not be going for long'. And I did, and I was ultimately the looser for it. Deception breeds deception, selfishness breeds selfishness and the lives all of those involved become more and more separate and inevitably more lonely.

* * * * * * *

I remember a while ago a national celebrity with some moral standing was asked to give the sermon at his local church. He was interviewed before the appointed Sunday, and asked if he was nervous.

"No, of course not".

"Aren't you a little afraid that you'll say something that does not match the church's beliefs".

"Not at all," he said, "they asked me to speak, and I will say what I feel. If it doesn't suit them, that is their fault, not mine. They should not have asked me to speak if they do not like what I'm likely to say."

In other words, if you believe someone is as you wish them to be, and they prove later not to be, that is not their fault, unless they set out to deceive you. This is why my trust is not in them, but is in my skill and experience at character assessment, and that skill and experience tells me that there are some circumstances when I would trust a person implicitly, but other circumstances, with the

The Self-Help Delusion

same person, when I would not. As in the old saying "I would trust him with my life, but not with anything valuable."

Outside of the domestic environment, socially and at work, it seems to me that we meet very few people that we can trust absolutely, with everything we are, with our hopes and fears, our strengths and frailties. It pays not to disclose too much of yourselves to too many people. We live in a critical world, and occasions can arise when in a crowd, the need to appear more important than we are, overtakes us, and we say things that were given to us in secret. We have all done it, and only fairly late in life did I learn that to disclose to some can be to disclose to all. And when that is realised before the disclosure rather than afterwards, that gives you strength because you are never surprised if the details come back to you through another channel. I do not view this as a betrayal by my friend, but perhaps a disappointing failure in my assessment of him.

You see, in the end, all your thoughts and the interpretation of all events are your responsibility, even the disappointing actions of others. For each person can only be, at any one time, what they are capable of being, and only make the decisions they are capable of making. If their choice suits us, we think they are 'good' and if it doesn't suit us, then we consider them 'bad'. It actually has nothing to do with them, or their behavior. Our judgment of their action is usually in relation to what we want of them. If there is any judgment at all, it is useful if we make it a judgment of what they want to achieve from that action, and how effective their action was in that regard, not whether or not it pleases us.

Generally, people do not have pleasing us as the motive for the action. Nor disappointing us either I suppose. If a work colleague does something that disappoints me, I work not on feeling the disappointment, but on determining the objective of their action. And sometimes I will ask them, "Tell me why you did that, it wasn't what I expected." From that you will generally find that that the reason had nothing to do with you, and that disappointing you was just a by-product and the furthest thing from their mind. Re-assess the person and their likely future actions in the light of what you find out, add to your knowledge of them, and you are likely to be less disappointed in the future.

There's a saying I'll paraphrase 'If someone disappoints you once, that's their responsibility, if they disappoint you twice, that's yours', because when they have demonstrated their rules of life, don't be too surprised if they follow them.

I have a friend who I see for an evening meal in the city on average about every two months. We've known each other now for some fifteen years. When we first began, I realised that she made at least three times more appointments that she ever kept. And I used to be very disappointed. She'd ring up the day before, or the same day and cancel. I used to get angry, because it was not at an inconsiderable cost in time and effort to me to arrange to make that appointment. But because she was interesting and pretty and I liked her, and she obviously liked me, I persevered with our friendship when many would have given up. This went on for several years.

And then I finally realised something very simple but very profound.

That is the way she is, she was following her rules, not mine. Her behavior had nothing to do with me, she just was that way.

And I had two choices, I either accept that she is like that and continue our friendship with a light-hearted approach to her unreliability, or reject her behavior as an affront to me as a person, and unacceptable, and not bother to see her again. I chose the former. And never for a moment have I regretted that choice. If I ever do, then I'll change it.

We still meet every 1-2 months, for lunch or a small shopping spree in the city. She has moved down the same routes of interests as I have, and supported and encouraged me to begin to do what I am. But the point I want to make about her actions is that she was building a reputation with me of being unreliable. That's fine. I'm a big boy, I can cope with that. But there's a far more significant aspect to her unreliability. She was building a reputation for unreliability with – herself. She is the one who suffered the most. Because if you cannot consider yourself as reliable and dependable, then what chance have you of considering that other people are?

Her loss was that by being offhand with her promises to another,

The Self-Help Delusion

she was offhand with her promises to herself because the world is a mirror which reflects back to you, an image of yourself. You start to think that other people are unreliable because you know you are. Then you will begin to draw unreliable people into your life in order to prove to yourself that the world actually is the way it appears to you. Since those days, she has turned around, and now we meet on the first arranged day/time, unless something totally untoward happens in our lives.

* * * * * * *

This brings me to another aspect of love and trust. Do you think it's possible to love someone that you do not trust? If your answer is no, then you are getting dragged back in your thoughts about love as being something that you get, rather than something that you give. Love wants nothing. If I want nothing from a person, why does it matter if I trust them or not, whether they only do what I want them to do or not, cannot affect the unconditional love I have for that person.

A person that I used to be very close to has decided recently that she does not wish to be in my company. I'd prefer that she did, but she doesn't. I still love her and always will but she chooses not to give me the opportunity to demonstrate my love, and I believe we are both the losers for that. Here's the point. I love her, but I would not trust her with my emotions, as she is too unreliable. I always felt that she could suddenly decide that I'm not the flavour of the month, and she has done just that. I can still say 'your will for you is my will for you' though not directly to her.

Now I'm not saying that that does not hurt. She is like a daughter to me, and she seemed happy with that relationship. I have feelings for her and it hurts when I am not in a position to express those feelings, as I would be if my own daughter were to put me out of her life. But her rejection of me has nothing to do with me. She has issues of her own, and she has decided that she doesn't want a father figure – which is what I was offering - in her life at this point. Deep down she knows that I love her she just doesn't want to accept it. She has found herself a good man, and seems happy with him, so why should I be troubled.

This is a very different way to see relationships and other people. I can give anyone my love but not my heart, because love wants nothing from them, but my heart does.

Once we realise that love/want/need/desire/lust are totally different things, life gets much easier.

Ego and Self-Worth

According to Freud's model of the psyche, the id is the primitive and instinctual part of the mind that contains sexual and aggressive drives and hidden memories, the super-ego operates as a moral conscience; and the ego is the realistic part that mediates between the desires of the id and the super-ego. To put it very simply, it's that part of our mind whose job it is to control the world we live in. Our self created world - though the ego doesn't know that. Ego is about control. And boy does it like to control; every thing and every body. We live in an ego driven world. We cannot resist sticking our human nose into absolutely everything. Nature and the way it works, another country and the way it operates, another person and what they wear, and just about every thing else. Throughout this book there are references to ego – the chapter on responsibility is all about ego. And also the section about should and shouldn't.

Earlier I suggested a model for the human being – Body, Conscious mind, Unconscious mind, Higher Self, and Freud created a model of the conscious mind / unconscious mind as having three parts, the Ego, Super-ego, and the Id. He was highly influential for the first fifty years of the last century, and still has his supporters. Other models and interpretations of the human process have been proposed since then, and each has its place in providing a basis to understand and predict human behavior.

The Ego is the controller. Wanting to control all that happens in our lives. And loss of control either real or perceived causes it to react in an attempt to regain control?

Only when we are not ego driven can we detach from the world, and watch the world and our lives happen in its perfection. When you make real all the time, and the key is, all the time, that you as an entity in this world are exactly as you are supposed to be, that you are perfect, that the outcome of your existence is not in question, that you do not have to be or do anything to have eternal life, that indeed this is part of your eternal life. Once you really 'get' that, the ego will be out of a job, and you no longer have the need to try to control the world.

It is very difficult to take the ego out of our psychological make-up, and I would not suggest we try. Note that there is a big difference between changing the world, and creating the world. If you decide that it is your life's purpose to change the world for the better, or create a commercial business in order to create wealth and spread wealth around, to be significant in the world and make a difference, it may not be ego that is driving that desire. It may be an altruistic attitude to the world and everybody in it. But it's probably your ego.

Ego, like most things, is neither good nor bad, it depends on whether you use it or it uses you. It all depends on the tasks you apply your ego to achieve.

****

Psychologists these days seem to be attributing many problems that people have to a lack of self-worth. Self-Worth to me (my meaning notice, not maybe the meaning give by other.) means what I think 'I' am worth. This begs the question, compared to what or who, as all things are relative in this world; in this case, relative to everyone else.

It seems a strange concept, because it's like saying that there are two separate parts of you, and one is standing in judgement over the other. This is nothing to do with intellect, or physical strength or any characteristics that the judged part possesses, but what the 'I' is deemed to be worth by that part of me that isn't the 'I'. Sounds very odd, but we do separate ourselves in our mind. That is part of the human condition, that we can recognise the 'I' as separate from the 'me'. A mouse is not aware that it is a mouse, nor an elephant that it is an elephant I suppose. But we are aware

The Self-Help Delusion

of ourselves as separate entities, and that the part that is aware can 'see' the other part that is doing the doing.

It's odd really, that one part of us seems to be judging the other part of us. When our internal dialog, or usually monolog says things to us like "I'm not good enough", or "I don't deserve it, this expresses the belief that I do not measure up to some standard or value that I have been told I should possess.

A background in the Christian religion or indeed any and every religion as far as I am aware, has a lot to answer for in this respect. I realise that this will go against the grain for many Christians, and I am not in any way opposed to Christ and his teaching. He was a 'son' of God, as are we all. But even there, in that innocent expression, there is a cause for argument. I just said "he was a son of God…". Christians would say that 'He was the son of God' and in that one word, there is a world of significance.

The bottom line seems to be that religions generally have mankind as less than perfect; in some way flawed. In the Christian religion there is the line "be thou perfect, even as thy Father in heaven is perfect". There is also the concept of original sin; that we are born in sin. Tricky to be perfect when we are born in sin. Also, thoughts like 'The sins of the father shall be visited on the sons, even unto the seventh generation'. So not only are we flawed simply by being, but we are doubly flawed because our father was too, and only by the grace of Jesus Christ can we be saved.

God, of course, disseminates that grace according to the dictates of his church – depending upon which church you happen to belong to. It seems like all religions believe this stuff – or similar ideas - with equal fervor. Get it wrong, be born into the wrong religion, and you are dammed before you start.

I cannot see these ideas as being empowering. We get these thoughts fed to us from an early age, and we unwittingly accept it into our belief system. That we are in some way worth less than we should be.

I'm spiritual, not religious. I believe in the essential goodness of man. That we are all 'sons of God'; that each soul is perfect, and that the outcome of my existence is not in doubt. It's not that we shall have eternal life; it's actually that we do have eternal life, and this is part of it. We have it. We don't need to earn it by being what God wants us to be. God has no wants. He/she/it is everything anyway. How could he want anything?

Again, the bible says 'Be thou perfect, even as thy father in heaven is perfect". That surly has the presupposition that we are not perfect? I prefer to see that as a misunderstanding. I think what was actually intended was "Thou art perfect, even as they father in heaven is perfect".

And we are told we are not. That's failure at the first gate. That's the gate of heaven on the way out of this life.

Why do we often have this desire, need, habit, trait, whatever, to consider ourselves less… less than 'good' enough I suppose. Why do we do it? Why do so many people consider themselves as 'not good enough'? Unfortunately, this idea of worthlessness diminishes our facility to be happy.

Doing our Happiness

With a new topic, I usually give my definition but this time it's a dictionary definition "a state of well-being characterised by emotions ranging from contentment to intense joy"
It isn't my definition, but it's a place to start so I'd like to pull it apart and examine the contents.

"A state of well being" has to be a mind state - a state of mind - not a physical state because it is "characterised by emotions ranging from contentment to intense joy". Emotions are held in the mind, not in possessions, or things of this world.

Most writings on happiness talk of 'finding' happiness. The problem with this approach – for me anyway – is that I have a belief that happiness is not out there to be found. It's not even inside you to be found. Happiness is not a thing to be found, like a lost cat or a CD. Happiness is a state of mind, the creation of which you alone are responsible. Once you have realised that state of mind, it accompanies you through all your doings.

* * * * * * * *

I think many people are unhappy for a variety of beliefs.

1. I have no right to happiness.
Some people have a belief that they have no right to happiness, created by the thought, 'how can I be happy when half the world is starving, killing each other, in wars, in pain, with pestilence and torture. What right have I to happiness when all that is going on?'

2. I don't deserve happiness.
Some people believe they have no right to happiness because 'I

don't deserve happiness after what I've done in my life' or 'what right have I to be happy when so many people aren't'. Guilt and shame of course encourage us to feel 'not good enough' and undeserving of happiness. We beat up on ourselves for things we have done in the past and we can't forgive ourselves because of what we have done.

NLP has the belief that 'everybody does the best they can from where they are in their life and state of mind at the time they do it'. And that includes you.

So whatever you have done, that was the best you could do, given your beliefs, fears, history, environment and state of mind at the time you did it and that should not debar you from having happiness now. Not to think that way is to fall into the trap that religions have set – 'be thou perfect even as they father in heaven is perfect', and since I'm not because of what I did, I don't deserve to be happy. Religion has a lot to answer for.

3. I cannot be happy until
Some people have a belief like "I can't be happy until ...." some person, or event, or purchase in their lives gives them permission to be happy. Naturally enough, when that person, or event, or purchase occurs, all is well for a time, and then the old feeling kicks in and they find another reason to put happiness off until the next person, or event, or purchase has come into their life. They are as happy as they can be with beliefs like that but after the cycle repeats for the nth time, it may dawn on them that they cannot be happy until… that happiness isn't happening, that they are getting older and that retail therapy or a new relationship or whatever they have been doing to find happiness gives pleasure and excitement for a time, but not happiness.

4. I cannot be happy until I have permission
Some people believe they need permission from something bigger than themselves before they can allow themselves to be happy. Transactional Analysis (TA) has the concept that some must have 'Permission' from someone bigger than themselves, who they can admire, or model themselves on, or respect; someone who seems

The Self-Help Delusion

to have this business of life sussed. We need that person to say, "It's ok to be happy. It really is. That is the way you were intended to live your live." It seems sad that, of all the invocations in the bible, no where can I remember it saying, "And be thou happy, even as thy father in heaven is happy." A sad omission that.

5. I cannot be happy in my present situation

It is not a useful to tell yourself, 'I cannot be happy after all that has happened to me' but I think you can say 'how can I be happy when I have a husband who gets drunk and beats me up every Saturday evening.'

This is a tough one because it would be difficult for anyone to be happy in this situation. If you change your belief from 'there is nothing I can do about it' and instead believe 'I need help and so does my husband because I am not loving myself by allowing myself to be beaten by my partner, and it is not loving to my partner when I allow him to beat me'. Then you can seek help from other people.

Your partner has problems and he is not going to move forward in his life until something changes the relationship between the two of you. The reason for your action is that since he does not realise he has a problem, and you do, you are the only one who can act to change the status-quo.

* * * * * * *

Of course these driving beliefs are usually not realised by the conscious mind. If they were, we would set out to change our beliefs. Few people ask themselves 'which beliefs do I need to change in order to be happy', because they do not realise that it is their beliefs that are preventing their happiness.

It struck me that a useful belief is that 'everybody has the right to be happy'. It comes with the territory as it were. It's an inherent part of being human. Mankind has unfortunately created societies which make happiness seem a favour, or just good luck or given to the rich and famous or not for the likes of me, or whatever limiting belief they have helped us create.

Some people have self pity
Some people think that the world will change in their favour if other people realised how unhappy it (the world) is making them. So they wander round with a bitterness and resentment because the world has treated them 'badly', and they deserve more than this, and 'I'm sure the world doesn't realise how unhappy I am'.

Many years ago, when I was very unhappy, I used to do self-pity and I was really good at it. If there had been an Olympic event for Self-Pity, I could have at least won a bronze medal. Needless to say, the world doesn't give a damn, and the only person who realises what their behavior means (to them) is themselves – eventually, and when they've hurt enough, they change. If they don't change, they haven't hurt enough. Of course, I wasn't the only person suffering. So were those with whom I had a close relationship, but I was so wrapped up in myself that I didn't notice them.

Then I had this nagging voice inside that said, 'You are worth more than this'. I started to read, and I became a recovering self-pityist, if there is such a word. I changed, and my current beliefs and this book are one result of that change. Once I changed my beliefs about being worthy, I gave myself the greatest present anyone can give themselves. I gave myself the gift of happiness. And of course, I was the only person who could.

If you change your beliefs about yourself and happiness, when you realise that it is a state of your mind, and that you are the only entity in charge of the state of your mind, you can decide to be happy.

That will no doubt seem a very flippant remark – 'you can decide to be happy'. It is that simple, but that does not make it easy. Most people's attempts to be happy don't work because they don't have a workable understanding of the nature of themselves and happiness, and happiness eludes so many people.

* * * * * * *

We are taught by our consumer society that happiness is found by the acquisition of goods and services. We have created our society because we are doing what we did when we lived in caves, and the

The Self-Help Delusion

strongest got the thickest skin to keep him warm. And at that level, warmth = Happiness.

Our western society cannot sell happiness because it's a state of mind created by a belief and cannot be weighed and measured. It sells us pleasure instead, and then pretends to us that it's the same thing. Our consumer society operates by consuming the earth's resources, and by teaching people to be consumers. I agree that whilst not essential, some degree of physical security makes the growth of the happiness mind-set far easier to attain. When starving in the gutter, it is perhaps more difficult to give yourself the gift of happiness.

I use that expression because it puts you in charge of your happiness. No one else is going to give you happiness. Your wife, your parents, your children cannot wrap it up as a Christmas or birthday present.

You are responsible for your happiness, indeed, we are each responsible for our own happiness. It's one thing we cannot give to another, no matter how much we love them.

To go back a little, physical deprivation does not prevent one being happy. I guess that the first men on the summit of Mount Everest were tired and cold and physically exhausted, but if asked at the time 'are you happy' I'll bet the answer was 'Yes'. Mother Theresa, for all her idiosyncratic behavior in the slums of India was, I don't doubt, blissfully happy. The first men on the moon in 1969, in spite of the extreme danger were no doubt totally happy.

It's true, they may have been. They were undoubtedly elated and on an emotional high but a few moments emotional high does not equate to happiness. Deep down, they may have been very unhappy with their life and themselves. Perhaps they took to climbing, or helping the poor or asronaughting in their search for happiness. Probably even they do not know the answer to that one.

I do not believe that a person's happiness is arrived at by things outside of them. There have been many rich people who have committed suicide when they got down to their last oil well. In fact, as I write, there has been a 17% rise in suicide in the countries hit the worst by the recession. These people were not paupers, but the loss of something was so important to them that they didn't want to live without it.

* * * * * * *

So, take on board the belief that happiness is a state of mind, and you have the freedom and the power to determine your state of mind. Well, if you don't, nobody else does. When you really believe that happiness can be yours when you make a decision about it, then you can give yourself permission to be happy. It's your choice.

If we have the belief that happiness is a decision, then we realise that we can decide to be happy and then we can make that decision to be happy. After all, if I believe I am happy because I believe that happiness is a decision and I've made that choice to be happy, who can really argue with that?

Some of course would say that's self deception, that I am only deceiving myself into thinking that I am happy. But here's the trick. I don't think I'm happy, because happiness is not a thinking process, it's a belief. I believe I am happy, in the same way that some people believe they are sad or unworthy or guilty or doomed, or controlled by others and the world, or not responsible for their emotions or whatever fantasy they have created. I have created the fantasy that I am happy. That seems to me to be far more useful to me than most of the other fantasies that people create to live their lives within. After all, some would say, self-development is only a more useful form of self delusion. Like I keep on saying WE ARE MAKING IT ALL UP.

Cause and effect
Can I really justify ignoring all the studies and research work that is undertaken by institutions and universities around so many topics and just ignore their findings. Even to me that can seem a somewhat arrogant approach.

However, when research is undertaken about any human behavior, there has to be a pre-supposition which drives the approach.

Well, there was a study of happiness in the US a while ago and the conclusions it arrived at were in keeping with the basic beliefs that the researchers had before the study. They were looking for a cause and effect that they already believed existed. They asked a group of people what they were doing when they were at their happiest.

That seems a neutral approach, but there are series of pre-suppositions in the question, even in the very asking of the question. The presupposition is that the actions that a person is performing has a connection with the happiness levels that that person experiences. They also asked people to associate activity with happiness.

Nobody would come back and say that it has no connection at all, especially when people have been taught throughout their life that some kinds of activity provides pleasure and we are taught to equate pleasure with happiness. Needless to say, the findings indicated that happiness accompanies a series of activities aimed to achieve a specific goal. Like I said, once you take a survey with questions, the very questions themselves cannot but lead to assumptions about the kind of answers you will get.

If you were to ask a number of 'happy and enlightened' people what it what provided their happiness, you might get a very different set of answers. Even if you were to ask a simple question like 'Why are you a happy person', it pre-supposes that there is a why, which comes back to a cause and effect process.

* * * * * * *

I suspect that most have realised that pleasure is not happiness, that they have recognised and enveloped all the people and events in their lives, that they work within the constraints their choices have put around them whilst at the same time, striving to change those constraints.

So they have accepted their lot?

You see, even that expression has so much to say about how we use words and expressions. That's because the words we use describe the way we are thinking. Taking that expression - 'so they have accepted their lot', to me the word 'accepted' has a sort of resignation about it. Like 'I don't really like it, but I'll accept it', and 'their lot' has a inevitability - a resignation, about it

It's a little like the words fate and destiny that we spoke of earlier, its outside of my control.

To me, the expression 'they have accepted their lot' is almost a religious 'that's what God intended for me in this life, that's my burden that I have been given to carry ' sort of feel about it. Happy people do not have that attitude, leastways, I don't believe they have. I certainly don't, because I realise that I am choosing my lot, at one level or another. I am actually the one in charge of my life, not some divine being with a grudge against me.

Another test for happiness is this: Can you remember a time when you had a feeling that you could describe as happiness? If there was any reason for this, then it wasn't happiness.

Happiness has no reason to be, it just is. If happiness had a reason to be, then it wouldn't exist if that reason did not exist; was not in place. Happiness does not vary with events, or people, or time, or behavior or surroundings or anything else.

I have an old car, and it's gave me a great deal of pleasure over the years. It's now ready to be scrapped and I have no money to replace it at the moment. But, and here's the point, I am no less happy without the car than I was with the car. I am sorry to loose it, and the decisions about how I spend my spare time will be different now I have no car, but I am just as happy without the car as I was with it. I want to replace it to resume my life style as before, and no doubt I will do that. Having a new car will not make me any happier, though I have no doubt it will give me pleasure.

And the same thing can be said about people. When I had work colleagues whose company I very much enjoyed. When one was off sick or on holiday, I missed the banter and the pleasure their company gave me, but I was no less happy in their absence. It made work that little less enjoyable than otherwise, but that was all.

Taking this belief to extremes, what about if a partner of ten years leaves you? It is very difficult to hold these beliefs in the face of great distress, either emotional or physical. But it does not make these ideas any the less valid. If you had believed yourself to be happy because of the relationship you had with your partner,

The Self-Help Delusion

then you would loose that happiness when the relationship ended. If you had decided to be a happy person because that was your choice, then your relationship ending would be a cause of your sadness, but not of your unhappiness.

Happiness and sadness are not opposites. When my son went to university, I was sad that he had left home, and that I could not experience his being around me at home every day. I was also happy that he had done well in his exams and was being accepted by and succeeding in the wide world.

So again, the bottom line is that happiness is a state of mind, and you have the freedom and the power to determine the state of your mind. Well, if you don't, nobody else does.

We've covered that Happiness is not dependent on outside situations like pleasure and excitement, but can we say the same about pain. Neither extreme emotion is connected to happiness. (See chapter on pain and suffering)

You can be happy but in pain or you can be experiencing pleasure but not be happy. The pleasure can mask an underlying unhappiness so that you don't notice it all the time. Some people are addicted to pleasure, sensory experiences, sex, drugs, rock 'n roll etc, but they may well not be experiencing happiness when they wake at 04:00 in the morning.

Lots of people in the caring professions believe that when a person behaves in a way in which they cannot allow themselves to behave, and operate their lives from a state of mind which they themselves cannot create, that there must be some underlying unhappiness or problem in that person's life. I don't go that way. I would say that they may well be very happy, they just happen to be into drugs and sex as well. They may have a problem, they may not. NLP has the expression 'People work perfectly' and when they have a problem it is that their behavior is not providing what they 'will' for themselves. They are acting in total harmony with the way they see themselves and the world. It's just that the world they have created for themselves is not assisting them to have what they will for themselves.

Now I'm not saying that when a person is into Sex, drugs and rock n roll that they are necessarily cool people fully aware of what they are doing, but for someone not into drugs and / or sex, it's very easy to believe that when another person is, that they are using them as mask for their basic insecurity, lack of self-esteem, social inadequacy or whatever other psychological defect that psychologists imagine that anyone not conforming to their idea of 'normal' must be suffering from. They may be, but I have learned not to generalise about people. They constantly surprise me.

Pain and Suffering

This is perhaps the most difficult topic to get your mind around. It covers matters that are not just of the mind, in terms of beliefs, but also of the body.

Pain and Suffering are two words which seem to be used interchangeably in the press and in day to day conversation. However, for me, very rarely do two words in the English language have the same meaning - the primary meaning perhaps, but not the secondary one. It seems to me that there is Pain, and there is Suffering.

Pain

For me, pain is caused by a physical situation and Suffering is caused by your thoughts about it. Another way to say it is that pain is an event, and suffering is your re-action to that event. In other words, pain is an experience and suffering is your thoughts about that experience. I realise that it seems very patronising, and trivialises the experiences that accompany intractable physical pain, but please go with the ideas for a time. Just accept for a while that suffering is our habitual re-action to pain.

If we first think about suffering, the definitions above lead us to the idea that there is no such thing as emotional pain only emotional suffering and many people would vehemently disagree with that notion..

A good place to start with this is to equate pain to physical events, and suffering to emotion events. Let's take something as common as toothache. Most people have experienced that at some point in their lives. The pain of course is physical. It is generally an indication that some part of you is damaged; not as it should be. With toothache, part of the tooth structure is damaged and the nerves are under pressure or exposed. It hurts like hell, and it's difficult to think clearly if it is intense. It's also right inside that part of the body where we think we reside - our head. If it's a broken toe, we can look at it more dispassionately. 'Oh your poor thing, how can I help you' as though it's not your toe. When the pain is in the head, it's more difficult.

And that's it really. The body is under stress, and that stress is taken on by the mind. We may sweat and feel faint - even actually faint if the pain is great enough. That's the body's reaction to the stress that it is under. I remember when in my twenties, I was head butted, or actually nose butted, by a youth wanting to come into our café after closing. I was driven to accident and emergency, bleeding like a pig, and had a stitch put in the end of my nose. I saw the doctor approaching with the needle and thread, and said 'Without anesthetic?' 'Not worth it' he said, and stuck the needle in. I went out like a light. I remember it very clearly, and it was over fifty years ago.

Obviously, if the toothache continues for several days at the same intensity, we can become ill as the body's immune system is under stress and we are more susceptible to the diseases that surround us at all times. Without treatment, the tooth will eventually become inflamed and rot out, and the nerves in that area will die and the pain will go away. Unfortunately this takes several weeks / months, and life can be very unpleasant while this is happening.

Fortunately of course, at least in developed countries, we have dentists who can treat the tooth, and avoid all that suffering.

No. I should have written, 'avoid all that pain', not 'avoid all that suffering'. We have so far described only pain, not suffering. It is so easy to use the words interchangeably, as we mentioned earlier.

Think of a woman giving birth. There is intense effort required to push the baby from the birth canal. The pain comes from the stretching of the vaginal muscles far beyond that necessary in normal physical activity. In this stretching, the muscles are damaged, and that creates the pain.

I guess there's not much suffering as such because of the purpose and relatively short duration of the birth process. Not only that, but the woman is too involved in the process to think about anything else at the time, and too focused on the outcome – a new life.

I was speaking with a friend of mine about her experiences at the birth of her first child. She said that immediately prior to and during the birth, she didn't suffer in the emotional sense that we are talking about. It was afterwards, lying in the hospital bed alone and separated from her baby. That was when the exhaustion and the hormonal changes took over and her emotions overwhelmed her natural self control. It was at that time when, though not in any real pain, she experienced suffering, and during birth, in real pain, she did not experience real suffering.

So suffering and pain can be considered as two separate experiences, sometimes accompanying each other, and sometimes arising independently.

Suffering

Suffering is always caused by our interpretations of physical events, and its extent is dependent on the meaning and significance we give to the event. Suffering can be experienced through many emotions: fear, anger, frustration, bitterness, aggression, sadness, etc. These are all reactions / responses to an event. With my friend I mentioned above, she said that self pity and feeling sorry for herself, emotions she doesn't usually entertain, were also there.

Fear is at the root of the negative emotions that constitute suffering. With my nose incident, I had no time to think much about the pain, it didn't last long, and I was unconscious for most of it. However, I remember having a tooth which ached like hell and needed treatment, for which I had to wait several days. Whilst waiting I found that a simple aspirin relieved the pain for several hours. Because I was in control of the pain, I was happy to wait long after the pain had returned before taking the next one. I haven't thought about it before, but actually, I had pain, but I did not really suffer, as I was in control of the pain relief. It's a feeling of helplessness or being a victim that creates the fear.

Here's a profound statement. 'Suffering, suffering in general, is created by the difference between the way you perceive it to be, and the way you want it to be'; the 'it' being any of your experiences in the world.

Think about it. If everything were the way you want it to be, could you experience suffering? I don't think you could. You could still experience pain though, and the only explanation is that pain and suffering is not the same thing. Man's problem is that everything is not the way he desires, and that causes his suffering. With my tooth experience, to some degree, I processed the pain as a challenge, or simply an experience which I had not created, but was almost welcome as I would not perhaps have the chance to experience it again, and my emotions would not be coming from fear, but actually love. Love of experience, of simply being here in this world, going through a very temporary opportunity to feel pain. We are always so afraid of pain because we are so often not in control, and we process it as undesirable.

All this reminds me of an acquaintance of mine who is a very complete, competent, intelligent woman, running her own company and, by her own admission, something of a control freak at work.

She has learned to process pain as a form of pleasure. After all there are many different types of nerves in the skin. A soft stroke excites one type of nerve as a cane stroke excites another. All that changes is the intensity and the sensation, and that in the latter, damage may be done to the body.

She used to attend - I'm not sure if she still does - a BDSM club and totally enjoys relinquishing control to her 'master'. He - and it doesn't have to be a he - will rope her up in physically demanding positions. She then likes to be lashed and then caned. This, she tells me, is a cathartic experience for her. She may finish the session with cane marks – not in places where her work colleagues will notice them - and she is happy with that. The damage to her skin will heal in a day or two. The experience is painful - extremely painful such that she may actually start tearing up. This is also ok, as she considers it a cathartic experience, an opportunity to release emotions which her natural self control doesn't allow her to release in normal relationships. She is in considerable pain but she has a safe word, and can stop the caning at any point. She generally chooses not to, but like me and my aspirin, she has control. She is in considerable pain, but not suffering as we define the words.

Ok. That may be an area of human behavior that you really don't want to know about, and I can understand that, but if we are thinking of pain and suffering, we cannot just think of behaviors of which we approve, and exclude those we don't. Don't forget that the early Christian saints used to scourge themselves, creating physical damage to themselves to show the intensity of their faith. And some of them have attained sainthood. These days we would consider them religious fanatics.

The division between pain and pleasure is not as clear as most people experience. After all, some people haven't had a good night out if they don't puke up down a side ally and quietly die in a corner the following day. I would consider that serious suffering, but they do it week after week.

So, in normal life - and I also don't consider the BDSM community as normal life - how do we avoid this inevitable suffering? Or, is suffering inevitable?

When you are suffering, this leaves you with two choices: change the way it is or change the way you think about it.

Change the way it is

My BDSM friend could change the way it is - being caned - but has obviously changed the way she processes the pain.

Take a more mundane example; when you have a shower in the morning, how hot do you have the water? Hot enough to be comfortable but not so hot as to be painful? Or even cool enough to be comfortable. If you begin with the temperature on cold, you probably consider it as unpleasant if you remember cold showers after games when you were at school.

So you turn up the temperature until it's comfortable. If you continue to turn it up, you will begin to suffer. Question is, at what point do you decide that the enjoyable experience of a warm shower becomes the painful experience of a hot shower? The point at which you decide this varies, not just between people, but will be different for you dependent on the attitude of mind you bring to it. I know that my son considers the thermal salt baths in Switzerland, which I adore, far too unpleasant to spend any time in. The point at which pleasure becomes pain, and pain becomes suffering varies with all of us.

The question is, do these thoughts work in perhaps serious but more mainstream events in life changing events like a broken leg, or the intractable pain of bone cancer,

I'm not for one moment thinking that the above analysis trivialises the problems encountered. The pain and the tears, the anguish and regret, the fear for the future and your responsibilities as bread winner etc, are real, and continue to be real. But one way or another, this is where you are, fair or unfair, just or unjust, and you have to get through it until time and the surgeon's skill bring back some semblance of normality to your life. You have no choice but to give the event and circumstances meaning - that's what human beings do. The question is; what meaning can we give it. See chapter on Meaning.

Whilst going through the process of recovery - very painful of course, and lasting for several months, a positive attitude of mind will reduce the suffering if not the pain. Reading about people who have lost part / all of their legs, or suffered other major accidents and led a relatively normal life afterwards helps to reduce the suffering. As the treatment progresses and the physical aspects of have been sorted, the next step is to move forward through rehabilitation, and to pick up your life making changes as necessary. This is an example of suffering pain as a result of a permanent change to the body.

Where do these ideas fit with emotional suffering? For example, take a relationship that isn't working for you – and probably for your partner also, if truth be told. The relationship may have grown over years into the way it is now. You may have changed your behavior to accommodate your friend/partner's wishes, and there comes a time when you realise that what you have become is not a true reflection of the way you want to be. Something has to change for you to be true to yourself.

In long term relationships, and in short ones for that matter, people play unconscious games with each other - (Games People Play - see Appendix) We learn to fit in with another's wishes, and there is a whole series of automatic re-actions to the stimulus that your partner offers. And these reactions are very difficult to break. After each altercation, you know that you should have said 'zzz' and yet at the time, you lapsed into the old pattern of behavior that does not instigate change. And then you start beating up on yourself for falling for the same trick you always have. And that doesn't help matters either.

The main thing to realise in these circumstances is that the only way you can change the relationship, is to stop reacting (re-acting) to your partner, and start responding in ways that serves you both. To do this, you need to give the stimulus you receive another meaning, and of course, this book is designed to help you to increase your choices in creating meanings in your life. All the arguing in the world is unlikely to change the other person. An intimate heart to heart might, if your partner realises that their seemingly innocent comments and remarks actually cause you problems and that another form of words could bring major improvements in your relationship.

In my experience, most people think that they are the innocent party, and that it is the other person who is 'the problem'. And of course sometimes they are. A violent reaction to anything said by either party is unacceptable. Some people – usually the woman – become victims in the relationship. This is a situation where the only solution is to get away from an abusive partner whatever the cost. There is little option but to leave, because, for whatever reason, the partner needs to 'sound off' every now and again, and a woman with low self esteem provides an ideal opportunity. They may say that it won't happen again, but it will. Some people and relationships are toxic and the only solution at that point is to move away from them.

Change your meaning
The other option is to change what you think about the cause of your suffering, change the way you want it to be.

I hope by now you have some understanding of the process that has caused you to create 'the way you want it', and consequently, to re-make that decision of 'the way you want it'. The eastern mystics have an expression 'to convert all your desires into preferences'. That is to say, you look to what you want, and ask yourself, do I really 'need' it to be that way? What is the benefit to me for it to be that way?

Say for example, the train you wish to catch is delayed. I know that I keep going on about trains, but they are a common experience for many, and a part of life that we as individuals have no control over. So the train is late and as a consequence, you miss your connection. This can cause you suffering one way or another. Anger usually follows hard on the heels of the fear you first have of the unknown future, the loss of control, the embarrassment you will feel when you don't get to the meeting on time, or what ever. Sometimes, anger follows so quickly, we don't even consciously register the fear.

So what can you do? You cannot make another train suddenly appear. You cannot change the fact that the train you wanted to catch has been delayed by 2 hours. You cannot change the way reality is presenting itself to you.

All that is left for you to do is to change your want to a preference. You would prefer that your train had not been delayed such that you miss the connection. But it has been. And when you only prefer that the train be on time, and it is not an absolutely 'must have', then you can rapidly begin to create other wants, other preferences; a plan 'B' as it were. After all, you will have to do this anyway; you just don't need to go through all the drama first; unless of course you need the drama. In which case, the train being late is a Godsend, as it provides you with the opportunity to experience the adrenaline kick that a good performance of anger and frustration can provide for you.

Bearing all this in mind will make it easier not to get wound up by events over which you have no control. However, it may well take some time for you to get rid of the skill of 'getting wound up'.

Being a commuter for the last twenty years has provided me with ample opportunities to practice the skill of not getting wound up, and I'm quite good at it now. Now I experience perhaps 5 seconds of resigned frustration, and then quickly create a plan 'B', assuming I hadn't even before the delay occurred. If plan 'B' falls

The Self-Help Delusion

through, I just laugh, because by then the hour, day, week, meeting or whatever is not going to happen the way I'd planned it, and I see it almost as a benign being playing games with me. And I process that as fun.

It can be fun as long as you have no urgent business to attend to. Sometimes it can be serious, but ultimately, very few appointments are that significant. Not really, in the grand scheme of things. With a mobile 'phone it's usually possible to inform those waiting that you will be late. Everybody these days realises that you being late is not necessarily a reflection of your organisational skills; except when they obviously are.

Sometimes I think that having learned these new skills, the experiences don't have to keep on being repeated. But the train operators are thorough in their training courses, and keep creating the circumstances for me to practice changing my needs into preferences.

Of course, if you don't wish to accept poor service and poor value for money as the norm, you are perfectly free – in the west anyway - to start a campaign and to walk down Whitehall with a banner proclaiming your beliefs. If you gather enough support, things can be changed. And that's cool, and all subsequent users of the service will benefit.

As I see it, it serves you ill to get steamed up about something that you are not prepared to actually do something about. Shouting at the traffic which is delaying you serves no useful purpose and raises your blood pressure, creates a negative state of mind for those around you, presents a less than effective you to the people you next meet and may well cause you to drive carelessly. The only approach that works is to accept that reality is not as you would like it to be, and move your mind to a conversation with your companions, or turn on the radio.

For me there was an occasion when an accepting attitude made life so much easier for me. My sister was looking after our 92 year old mother for the last 10 years of her life. A while ago, my sister was taken into hospital, and I had to take over her role in my mother's house, literally at a moments notice. My response surprised me. My work allowed for some flexibility, and my life changed for three weeks while I did the job of carer. A great learning experience, as my mother was not always in the moment, and it would have been very easy to have become frustrated by the repetitions needed to communicate with her. And for the first few days, I did get mildly frustrated. Each time I 'lost it' I came back to the present moment, and looked at it from my mother's position; incontinent, half blind, half deaf, almost immobile, and housebound with dementia, then suddenly, my frustration seemed so out of place, petty and irrelevant to her situation or mine really. Even at the time it was happening, I considered this a wonderful opportunity for personal growth. I knew that I was growing into a totally new role, with an opportunity to test my beliefs, realisations, and patterns of behavior. And I surprised and delighted myself with the ease and acceptance I felt about my new role. I did not volunteer for the opportunity, but when it presented itself, even though I pretty much had no choice, I was delighted with my responses to the challenge.

* * * * * * * *

Let's go another step more deeply into personal situations; a personally serious situation - terminal cancer for example. Where do these ideas take us?

This is often truly difficult. To face this situation, to experience the best quality of life requires a mind-set that few people know about, arrive at or even desire to arrive at. It requires enlightenment and a serious change to most people's existing belief. Not just to accept the pain and fear, but to actually see it as a 'good' thing. That's difficult, because we have been taught all our lives to resist pain, and here I am telling you to accept it, and even to love it.

And yet, ultimately, that is the only way to live an acceptable life in the face of constant physical pain and the fear of death. There's little doubt that the more you fight it and dwell on it, telling yourself how much you don't want it, the more you accentuate the difference between reality as you are experiencing it, and the way you want it in your head. And it's that difference that creates your suffering.

The Nature of Emotions

Emotions often come to us unannounced and the negative ones are generally unwelcome. They are created deep down in the unconscious mind, outside the control of the conscious mind. We can learn to cope with them, realise where they come from; respond rather than react to the energies they feed to the mind, but ultimately, only a change of belief will provide you with a more serene approach to the vagaries of life.

The negative emotions can be fall under the general headings of: Anger, Sadness, Fear and Guilt. I'll discuss each in turn to perhaps better understand their origin.

Anger
Last week I became very angry at work. A team colleague was having difficulty with a telephone caller, and she was left to struggle. I knew that the manager was allowing that to happen, and I have a major problem watching and listening to another person suffering. My natural instinct was to help her, but I knew that was not what my manager wanted. I became angry that she was allowed to suffer, and he refused to intervene. After any difficult and emotional conversation, we need, the team needs, to unload the emotion with colleagues. As we were 'unloading' the emotion of the moment, he was rude and offhand to the team, as in 'get back to work'. These two events triggered an uncharacteristic and disproportionate reaction in me. It was definitely a re-action, not a response.

I told him that he and I should have a little chat. Now. In the office.

I was physically shaking when I told him that his behavior was not in keeping with his position, that it was his job to placate angry customers, not ours and that if he ever spoke to us like that again, we, the team would report him to HR.

He apologised. Bottom line was that we shook hands, and our relationship has not been harmed by the event and we both learned a lot from it.

When my manager, who is a decent man, allowed a friend of mine to suffer and threatened the team and me by his rudeness, I was afraid. That fear became anger, and I couldn't hold it in. It was so strong that my sense of humour, which I never loose, was lost. Fortunately, I have been very well socialised and I use words to express my emotion, never violence, provided I can verbalise my emotion. On that occasion I was allowed to but had I not been, I'm not sure what I would have happened. It is a very long time since I felt such anger.

There is the expression, 'I am no more the anger that I feel, than the sky is the cloud that passes across it. Problem is; it's not that easy to discount a deeply felt emotion.

I believe that all beliefs and behaviors originate from one of two places; either Fear or Love. The incident above was a useful learning opportunity for me, even if it was unwelcome at the time, and very clearly came from fear. After all, if one had no fear of anything, why would one get angry?

Again, let's go to an extreme. Take for example an emotion closer to home - literally. What about the emotion that the husband feels when he finds out that his wife has been unfaithful to him or a wife when her husband has been unfaithful to her.

There is likely to be a mass of emotions arising. Most of the emotions will be around anger; anger at being belittled, at being cheated, at being diminished, at being lied to. That anger will originate in fear. The fear of being left on your own perhaps in later life, and having your life unexpectedly changed and the fear that the loss of intimacy that you feel will perhaps never be replaced. You will feel disappointment at the loss of a planned future, and anger perhaps with yourself for not seeing it coming.

I think after your initial anger, the depth of your feelings will depend on how you processes your partner's decision for a change of circumstances, and that will depend on how much you love

The Self-Help Delusion

them. And I know that that is easy for me to say, but not so easy for you to do.

In the end, it depends on whether the love you have for your partner is greater than your own fears about yourself. It's doubtful if you will be able to separate the anger you feel towards your partner, from the fear you feel about your new situation.

However, remember that I defined love as 'your will for you is my will for you.'

I've realised that we cannot always be for another, what that other wants for themselves. I see a beautiful woman, and I may want to be part of her life so much that it hurts. But I cannot be what that woman wants for herself. That is a fact of nature. All I can do is to be for her what she wants me to be for her; a work colleague, a coffee friend, a confident, a surrogate father, or perhaps nothing. I have to be only what that person wants for herself, and I have to ignore what I want for myself. Her will for her is my will for her. I cannot be a larger part of her life than she chooses to allow. If your wife leaves you, a wife of perhaps 30 years, the only way to find solace in this situation is to keep reminding yourself of this statement. Every time the feeling of being let down, anger, bitterness, disappointment, fear, frustration come rushing into your mind, remind yourself of this belief, and the knowledge that the partner you love is living her life the way she wants to. It's just unfortunate that she does not want it to include you.

For the vast majority, the personal fear about their own future overwhelms their love for their partner. It's not that easy to get over the hurt and suffering. It takes time to restructure your life, and whilst that is happening, you are suffering. As I said, just because it's simple doesn't make it easy.

I'm suggesting that the suffering will be less once the person left behind has decide what they really mean by love. Most people have a strong element of 'what's in this relationship for me' in their 'love' for their partner. It's the loss of this element of the relationship which generates the fear which leads to all the other negative emotions. In the end, it all comes down to beliefs.

The effective long term resolution of negative emotions like anger does not lie in the area of psychology; it lies in the area of philosophy.

It seems to me that a shortcoming of 'Anger Management' courses is that they do not necessarily address the reasons why a person feels angry Anger management courses are largely only Elastoplasts to prevent the anger from bleeding into the world. The only long term solution is to change beliefs and then the behaviors so that we don't keep cutting ourselves in the first place.

People feel angry because some aspect of their world is not as they wish it to be, and they are afraid. That's as a result of the beliefs they hold about themselves and the world. Change their beliefs, and their world will change. Indeed, until their beliefs change their world cannot change. Suppression of anger is not good from a physiological point of view.

It's easy to think that if you were to acquire the sort of detachment that I am speaking of, where you have no great desire for anything in particular, you would be emotionally dead. But that misses the point. You can take joy in the prospect of an event happening, and also in it's actually happening, but not fall into deep melancholy if it does not. As I said, I have been called a cynic, but I think that is untrue, given the meaning that most have for the word. To many it has overtones of bitterness and injustice and I don't have that.

Personally, I think that anger largely hinders my growth. My father used to say "If you are in the right, you have no need to get angry, and if you are in the wrong, you have no right to get angry." That's great, but in reality, it doesn't seem to quite work out like that. Anger is one reaction to the fear we feel when some part of the way we define ourselves is being taken away or made fun of or violated.

Earlier I said that all thoughts come from either love or fear; not only all thoughts, but all behaviors too. Sometimes we act without thought as we discussed earlier. Anger comes from a fear of being personally threatened. If I offend someone, and he gets angry, it's easy to think that it wasn't because he felt personally threatened. There was no threat to his person, but that depends on how you define person.

The Self-Help Delusion

We define ourselves by a whole range of things: our values, thoughts, beliefs, ideas, opinions, memories and history, our intellect, by our use of language, our jokes, our tastes in everything, our approach to life, our body and its appearance, our football team, and a host of other things.

We don't realise these things are part of the way we see ourselves, but when any of them are threatened, we feel fear. The more closely we connect our personal value or personal worth to these characteristics, the more we instinctively defend them in the face of a perceived attack.

There is a quote, "To the degree that you are concerned what another person thinks of you, you are owned by them." The significance of the opinion of others is different with each of us. The more 'grounded' you are, the less it matters. With young people who do not know what they are, they define themselves by what their peer group determines that they should be. We conform to the group that we spend the most time with. And after a while we become as the group requires us to be.

Or we leave the group. I've done many different jobs since I left school, and each for a number of years. Quite long enough to adopt the skills and attitudes necessary to be in the 'in crowd'. Needless to say, I realised that those attributes I adopted were not me, but only a different set of clothes in which I can feel comfortable. I don't define myself by what I do, but by what I am. Of course part of what I am is what I am writing at this moment.

Once you understand and realise your own worth, you no longer need to defend it. Others can say as they will, but you know that no one else is in competition to be you. You are the perfect you, there never was anyone quite like you, and there will never be another quite like you. You are perfect, and you do not have to do anything to remain perfect.

When that becomes part of your reality, real anger cannot exist, because you know that nothing outside of yourself, apart from physical danger, can threaten you or harm the real you that you now know yourself to be.

We have choice in the world as to how to respond to the various stimuli that the world offers us. I would not say that anger is always a negative response, childish, unnecessary, uncalled for etc as many would. I think that anger, controlled anger can be of value on occasions where all the other behaviors in your tool cupboard fail to get the response you feel to be necessary. It's a bit like smacking kids. I wouldn't rule it out, but it has to be used under control and for win-win reasons where time is of the essence, and reasoning isn't working.

I think that the more times you use anger to get your way with children, the less effect it has. You get an "Oh, Mummy's off on one again" sort of response.

The response of anger, when under your control, can be used as a tool, like humour, to move you though the social necessities of the 'real' world. When out of your control it becomes an instinctive, re-action to a perceived threat to the fragile entity that you used to see yourself as being, and generally the outcome is not useful...

When you are totally comfortable in your own skin, you won't even feel anger.

In fact, anger is a valuable aid to noting your progress in personal development, or the journey of the soul, or however you want to describe what we are doing here.

I had an experience a few days ago at the supermarket. I was standing in a queue which divided into four further along. A woman joined the queue further up one of the channels, and was served before me. This annoyed me. I didn't say anything, and I did actually stop and think that if this feeling comes from fear, which part of me feels threatened. Was it my ego, my sense of importance, my sense of fairness? What was I going to loose by her action. I wasn't short of time, the shop wasn't closing, and I was next in the queue anyway. But I felt affronted by her actions.

As I said earlier, suffering - and anger is one manifestation of suffering - suffering is the difference between the way it seems to you, and the way you want it to be. If all is as you want it to be, why would you get angry and suffer? Clearly, being bumped in the queue was not as I wanted, and anger resulted. Perhaps I have some way to go.

The Self-Help Delusion

* * * * * * *

Therein lays the basic problem of mankind. We are all afraid. We are all afraid because we have been taught to be afraid; taught by frightened parents, by frightened friends, by frightened teachers, by a frightened society. We have been taught to believe that we are not enough, that we are in some way less than we should be. That unless we perform in a certain way, or believe certain things, a fate worse than death will befall us. Half the advertisements that are beamed at us through one medium or another are pandering to our basic fears.

Our anger is directed outward when someone or something appears to threaten us. The fear we feel when things seem out of our control. We feel that as long as we can control the environment we live in, we will survive. By environment I include other people and their actions.

I spoke about abdicating control in the chapters on pain and suffering.

Of course the reality is that we will survive anyway, except in the direst of circumstances. Even then, to go all esoteric on you, our soul will survive us, even after the death of our body. So fear leading to anger is rather an unnecessary emotion, and all the ill-considered thoughts and actions unnecessary.

The question is, 'How can we avoid feeling anger' not 'How can I stop being angry".

These questions may seem to elicit the same answers, and so they do, but the way you say things is the way you think about it. There is a world of difference between feeling anger, and being angry. The first detaches you from the anger, and recognises it as a feeling which will pass its way through you. The second puts you and anger as synonymous.

That's the key really. When your thinking changes, so do your words and when your words change, so does your thinking.

I think that it's inappropriate anger that should be avoided. I say inappropriate because some display of anger, as I said earlier, can be useful as long as it is under conscious control. And appropriate means in keeping with the here and now stimulus that prompted the anger rather than a release of pent up anger because of something from another part of your life or your past history. Many people seem to be on a 'short fuse', and an insignificant stimulus prompts an outpouring of the anger, pent up as it were behind the dam of social acceptability, to say nothing of legal consequences,

I spoke earlier about inconsiderate people. Somebody bumps into you on a crowded train. A customer is curt and rude at your checkout. Somebody 'steals' a car park space you had earmarked for yourself.

Most people believe that any of these events have something to do with them. And you can stick with that belief if you wish, but I think that a far more useful belief comes from the realisation that the person on the train doesn't know you. You just happen to have a body in the way when she wants to get off quickly to catch her next train. The customer doesn't know you at the checkout. He is just annoyed that his partner has sent him out for eggs whilst he was listening to his favorite Mozart concerto, and you weren't even in the picture when that Ford escort took 'your' space; all that person saw was a car – assuming that he saw anything other than the space.

Anger directed at an innocent is bullying. Most anger has nothing to do with the person that it's directed towards. People only get angry when it's 'safe' to get angry. They find a person who will not fight them back, either because they don't have the verbal skills, or because the relationship is unequal in some way.. This is when one party has something to loose and the other doesn't. They may be in fear of loosing their job or a prospective job. It is nothing to slag off a shop girl, because if she complains to the manager, she may be seen as incompetent or rude. The customer is a bully, and there is little that the shop assistant can do about it. Unfortunately we all know that bullies do not pick on big people - big people physically or big people intellectually or linguistically.

So after the next time you feel angry, you could ask yourself if your feelings are proportionate to the event that triggered them. Think if anger is the optimum way to get what you want, in a win-win way with the other person - otherwise it is not loving that person, and not a true reflection of what I believe you wish to be in this world.

* * * * * * * *

Sadness

Sadness has degrees of significance to the person feeling it. It can range from the trivial – I wanted to take the dog for a walk but its raining, through to the grief on the loss of a loved one – pet ot person.

Grief

It might initially seem strange that we use the expression 'Good Grief'?

It's difficult to process grief as a good thing. It's perhaps because the wisdom of the ages, that's the ages where the expression was first created, gave us to realise that grief, in all its forms, is a wake up call to higher thoughts.

Let's take this to an extreme. My only sister died in 2009. How could I process that event?

We have relationships in this life. Through these relationships we realise what we are, and what we want to become. 'We' used here is the worldly we, not the spiritual we; the spiritual 'we' never changes. We become we by the relationships we have. Without them, and memories of relationships we once had, we do not have a presence in this world. Remember the expression 'without that which I am not, even that which I am is not?

My sister and I had a relationship. I'd known her all my life. When she died, part of me died with her because she was part of the way I created my definition of myself. I had to start to redefine myself in the light of her absence, because the part of her that was also part of me was no longer in this world. The memory of her, the memory of the relationship I had with her is still there in my memory, but it is static. And I am dynamic. We are all works in progress, not static entities. When people say 'you must move on' that can be taken as a physical description of an emotional process.

That relationship which is part of your self-definition has ended, and you have to put together the other pieces of you, to redefine yourself, so as not to leave a gap, and you do that by creating a different pattern, a different self.

People say, and experience has taught me, that we do 'put ourselves together' again, though we are never the same as we were. We cannot be, because part of what used to be us is now missing.

The explanation I've given is only a model to provide one rational explanation of what is happening in our unconscious mind. It doesn't take away the hurt, fear, anger, regret, guilt and all the other feelings that may overwhelm us after a loss.

The common perception is that 'time will heal', and I guess it does. I'm suggesting that it takes time for the mind to redefine itself in the light of the loss, and that the greater the loss, the longer to heal.

There is no obvious correlation between the apparent magnitude of the loss, and the time taken for the mind's healing to take place. Some people get over a loss more quickly than others would, given a similar relationship loss. If you are living happily with someone, and they are a significant part of your daily life, the relationship you have with them will be more important, a greater part of your self-definition and the loss will be greater than if they lived in a different part of the country, and you rarely see them.

Our mother died in 2002, then living with my late sister who looked after her. They lived some 8 miles away from my house, and I saw them every week. Our mother was nothing like as major a part of my life as she was of my sister's. She was 93 when she died, and had not really been in this world for some years before that. It might sound very hard and unfeeling, but I had no grief about her death; absolutely none. She was my mother, and I'd always had a good relationship with her, and yet I felt nothing when she died. I think I'm normal, but sometimes my lack of feeling troubles me.

I loved my mother – as in 'her will for her was my will for her'. She was 93 years of age, mentally not in this world, and certainly not going anywhere in this world, and she didn't have much impact on my way of life.

Because of this, she had ceased some time ago to be a developing entity in the way I think of myself. My memory of her as a mother and the relationship I had with that memory was already static because in fact she was static, unchanging in her last at least 10 years. I had already redefined myself in this life as though she were no longer in it.

All those memories of her are still stored in my head, all my early years, when I was growing up, when she looked after me. Of course I have not lost those memories; they will always be with me if I want to recall them. I guess I could get depressed if I consciously spent much time recalling them, going over old ground, to see my mother as she once was, a young mother in a productive life in our family business. But I don't. I'm not really into nostalgia

And that alone of course saves me a lot of grief – literally. Some people are closer to their feelings than others. Some actually enjoy the feelings of grief, and they will go back in their mind for years to come, and feel bad about an event that has long since passed. Initially, I think that can be useful as it helps to reposition the aspects of your life, your self definition, restructuring yourself to take account of the loss. Going back over it and over it seems to me like self indulgence. It can get very addictive, like self pity does. Once the mind has restructured, going back over it is self pity, and serves no positive purpose.

I was a master of self pity. If it was an Olympic sport, I could have won the self pity Gold Medal for England. It took me about 20 years to realise the following: you can be happy or you can be miserable, and the rest of the world doesn't give a shit.

Shortly after that, I gave up self pity, and apart from the odd five minutes, I don't do it anymore. The rest of the world will not correct what ever has made you decide to be miserable, you have to do tht yourself.

* * * * * * * *

I remember my line manager once said to me that I am cynical about management. I said why single out management, I'm cynical about everything. That's not a cynicism with bitterness, just a realistic - that's my realistic you understand - approach to the difference between what people say and what people do. I used to get very disappointed when things I had looked forward to didn't happen. I came across the expression 'don't plan your disappointments so well.' and I realised that if it happens, I'll be delighted, and if it doesn't, I shall not be too surprised. I'm over seventy now, and very little surprises me anymore. People do what people do. Sometime it coincides with what they say, and sometimes not. Either way I'm not greatly surprised because both possibilities seem to have an equal chance of coming to pass. The only way I can be sure something is going to happen is when it has.

The object is not to eliminate emotion, but to reduce its impact on your un-chosen behavior. If events cause you to feel sad, then the belief that to stay with that sad emotion is your choice can be very useful to you. Time spent in sadness is not always wasted or unproductive time. Sadness helps us to structure and give meaning to events that we do not like.

* * * * * * * *

Fear

One of my deep set attitudes is a fear of authority. That was set in place, I believe, when I was about six years old – late 40s - the whole class was caned on the hand because of the behavior of a few other children. I had done nothing wrong. Suddenly, this place and the people there who had been nurturing and loving turned on me and caused me pain. It was a traumatic event. It hurt me physically, and I suffered emotionally, such that I have never totally overcome this childhood fear of authority.

* * * * * * * *

Guilt

There are graduations of expectation of something happening when somebody says it will.

I have been in the world, and in industry long enough to have been disappointed so many times by the blandishments and promises by management and friends, that I automatically have

The Self-Help Delusion

a 'perhaps so' attitude. I'm happy to believe that the manager or CEO believes they are telling the truth, it just turns out to be an untruth. That's not to say that I don't embrace the project or prospect wholeheartedly, but for my own intellectual and emotional security I always have a 'plan B' in my mind. 'Yes, yes, yes, cool, but what if it doesn't'. Maybe my training as a programmer has helped with this, where all the possible outcomes have to be recognised and provided for, even if it's just with a warning message or error message. I cannot go wholeheartedly for anything because there are always alternative possibilities. In some ways I envy those younger people who have a crystal clear direction without a thought for the notion, 'but what if it doesn't'.

What I am suggesting is that whilst we can learn to handle emotions as they are generated in the unconscious mind, by counseling and therapy and psychological analysis of one kind or another, we can change our beliefs from a philosophical point of view and not generate such intense feelings in the first place.

When we build a philosophy, we can realise and acknowledge negative emotions and choose to change our mindset about them, whilst taking huge pleasure in the positive emotions. I'm not suggesting for one moment that it's easy to do that. Suffering is still suffering, but when you apply the ideas of love that we have spoke about, ideas of forgiveness, or even that there isn't really anything to forgive, ideas of changing a desire from 'need' to 'want' to 'preference', ideas that we are all doing the best we can in this life, that we are all saying the world the way we see the world at that moment, that words are only said from where a person is at that moment, and not necessarily a reflection of that person's total belief system, emotions can become easier to acknowledge and become useful energies, not destructive ones.

Over a period of time, these ideas can reduce the suffering of small personal disappointments such as I suggested earlier, but it is more difficult for a person who has been made redundant and realizes that his whole life has become dominated by the job he no longer has.

We can consider that all members of all societies are 'trapped' in the lifestyle they are living. Sometimes that lifestyle has been bequeathed to them as a child; in the third world, a farmer's son will be a farmer – there's not too much choice. In second world societies, there is more choice, but it usually involves travel to another country to college, or university, and then to relatively well paid work.

In our first world society, we have more choices in how we create our lives and not too much effort and family upheaval is required to change them. It's sad that we have a section of our society who do not see it this way, and consider themselves trapped even before they have started their lives. And of course, for them, their reality will follow their belief.

The lifestyle chosen or inherited, for all people, is often supported by factors outside of their control; famine, pestilence, and civil unrest for those in the third word, economic circumstances, managerial decisions and social changes for those of us in the 1st world. Any of these causes, along with lots of others, can create an upheaval in our otherwise ordered and controlled life.

I have learned that unconditional love is not an emotion, it's a decision. I know that disappointment is only temporary - there's a great line from a song by Jewel, 'all things are temporary if you give them enough time'.

I still have the capacity to feel negative emotions, but I am now far more aware when I'm feeling them, and I haven't 'lost it' for a very long time. Likewise, I haven't cried in hurt for a very long time either.

I do the positive stuff so much better and more enjoyably than I used to. I still want what social convention and my morality will not permit me to have but I realise that it is a want, not a need, and my life will continue happily without it.

I cry, or at least dampen my eyes more easily than I used to, and so often at such little things, particular beauty and competence and achievement. That reminds me, and here's a secret.

In 2004 I watched Maria Sharapova win the Wimbledon tennis championship, and I just cried as I watched her. All the things that generate my tears were there. She was a beautiful 17 year old girl / woman. Blond, baby faced yet 6ft tall. Such grace and elegance, such self belief in one so young, such total control of herself and her environment. Great skill and determination, all wrapped up in so gorgeous a package. And her mental approach to her mistakes was so mature. When she made a mistake, an unforced error, she would walk to the back of the court and pause for a moment or two, to analyse what she did wrong, why the shot selection or execution wasn't right, and learned to do better next time. No beating up on herself, no histrionics, no smashing of rackets, no complaining to the umpire; just a quiet conversation with herself, her unconscious mind, to do better next time.

Afterwards she simply said "I just told myself that the power was in me and if I put my mind to something, I can do it."

Man, God and Religion

I think that religion plays a greater part in our life than even the non religious realise. As you may have gathered by now, I'm not an advocate of religions. I am the son of a father who, for a period of his life before I knew him, was a lay preacher for the Methodist church. My father was a Christian, in terms of living the Christian life, and was not too interested in the finer points of any branch of Christianity. In that respect, I have learned my lesson well; I must have acquired my beliefs by osmosis, because he never spoke of them directly.

I realise that for devout followers of a particular religion, my truths that follow could be offensive. That is to say, followers could be offended. There is nothing offensive in the words themselves, they mean nothing as we realised earlier, but taken together with a person's truths, and one of their truths is that they known the truth, my words will be considered as blasphemy. And, you see, that is the problem.

Religions uses fear to control, to encourage people to do as they – the leaders of the religion – wish. Hell and Damnation if you don't and a secure place in heaven if you do - do whatever has been deemed as required of you by God. Of course, it is only men doing the deeming. There is a common idea among therapists, that a client talking to God is ok, but when God talks to the client it is time to be concerned. And all of the deeming is as a result of God talking to man, or more accurately, man believing that God is talking to them.

Most religions have created a dependency on their religion, and decreed that an intermediary is required to connect you with God. The leaders of the religion are in some way different to you, higher in the pecking order, as it were, in the divine administration. They have a fast track to God and his desires. What has happened, and it began a long time ago, is that man has created the same infrastructures in religion he has created on earth. Of course that serves individual needs for position and power, the same as hierarchies do on earth. In the Catholic Church, men have created the dependency that when you are dying, you should do so in the presence of a cleric, or have received the blessing of a cleric not long before, or at least since you have had an occasion to 'sin' – their definition of what God would consider a sin. Take the case of women; damned from the start in the Garden of Eden story, and still damned today in many religions. Even the Catholic Church, though it has dropped many of its more idiosyncratic restrictions, still does not consider women to be equal to men. Still believes that half of the world's population is not as good as the other half; in some way spiritually inferior.

I do not believe that God made women to be spiritually inferior to men. Nor did he make lesbians and gays inferior either. Gays are simply not allowed in most religions, and women are often given only the minor, though admittedly necessary roles in the religious infrastructure. In most religions, they have no chance of attaining any significance. Talk about the glass ceiling that is the cause of so much female frustration in the city and industry. Many women who are fighters in life and business and believe in equality for all, still follow a religion that denies this basic human right of equality before God. Does that make sense to you, because it doesn't to me? Needless to say, the religions that have this idea were created by man.

I'm no advocate of the more extreme examples of the woman's rights movement that sees all men as potential rapists, but man has imposed on religion the prejudices, social mores and social hierarchical structures that were prevalent when these religions were created. And with few exceptions, they have not changed.

The sacred documents of most if not all religions have sections that most adherents to that religion consider to be unacceptable in the western world. We choose to ignore those parts of the 'religious law' that seem out of place, and follow only those dictates that don't interfere too much in our way of life. The fundamentalists

The Self-Help Delusion

of course take every aspect of the 'law' and interpret it literally. Recently, the Taliban in Afghanistan carried out the 'extremes' of the Quran and subjugated the people, beating women with sticks if they dared show an ankle or a man if his beard was not the right length. I cannot believe that this is other than nonsense.

I don't believe that these are God's decrees, God's wishes or God's judgments. We have truly created a god in Man's image, and not, as God said He had done, created man in God's image.

I had to smile last time I was in Oxford, when I noted some graffiti on the wall of a house. "Those who are devoted to the dogma of any religion are committing intellectual suicide." Maybe you get a higher form of graffiti in Oxford.

In the light of all we have talked about, most religions makes no sense. Who told these people that all that they do is God's will? I guess they read it in their holy books, and were told it by their religious leaders, and because many people like to have some certainty in their lives, they chose to believe it.

Religions take away the scary uncertainty of not knowing. Someone older, more learned, has told me the truth about God and Man, and that saves me from having to work anything out for myself.

These are Man's gods, and Man's religions, and I believe they play no part in your spiritual existence. Leastways, they certainly don't in mine. In fact, I believe that religions have actually driven people away from the contemplation of the spiritual. And that's because deep down, right down inside, they know that religions and the nature of the Gods we have created do not make sense. They are at variance with their own experiences. They know this and want no part of it. And given the nature of the Gods they are asked to believe in, I don't blame them.

Religion became an academic study. People spend their lives analysing the texts, the translations, the languages. And they lost the plot. (God save me from the experts.) The Gospels were not written by the people who were there at the time. They are the Gospels according to … whoever. Often hear-say, and only a selected set of the 'holy' writings produced around that time, the bible is not a definitive statement, it is a selected series of writings, added to and subtracted from, translated and translated again to suit the intentions and beliefs and social aspirations of the people of the time.

I remember that the Bible I was brought up with had the commandment 'Thou shalt not kill.' The later version I noticed has it changed to 'you shall not commit murder'. It's a small point I guess, but 'kill' does not allow for interpretation. 'Murder' does; one man's murderer is another man's freedom fighter. And that's only one small point I happen to have noticed – no longer being an avid reader of fiction.

The Gods created by most religions, those that actually have a deity, they have created a small god, full of anger and judgment.

One only has to play the Chinese whispers game to realise that by the time the message has been passed on a few times, in some case the whole meaning, and always some subtlety, is lost. Some people make their life's belief from some small aspect of a historical translation that was written a generation after the event.

A person's religion is as a result of chronology and geography; when they were born and where they were born.

I remember the old joke about a catholic cardinal, who went to heaven – as all cardinals surly must – and since he could do anything he wanted, and he had an eternity to do it in, he spent seven earth years studying the language in which the original holy texts were written. He then sat down for the next few years and studied the original texts. One morning St Peter heard a roaring and a ranting and a sobbing coming from the library. He rushed to find out what was causing it. The Cardinal was pacing around in obviously agitated state. "What's wrong?" asked St Peter.

"They missed out the 'R'. They missed out the 'R'."

"What do you mean they missed out the 'R'?"

With tears in his eyes, the Cardinal looked up. "The original word was 'Celebrate'"

Personal Spirituality

The last topic I want to look at in this book is Spirituality. Its one aspect of life that many people have either never thought about or they have shied away from, even more than from the words God or Religion. Along with politics and sexuality, religion and spirituality are the topics that are not up for discussion at polite dinner tables. And that's a pity, because they are the only ones that really matter.

Some think of spirituality as being either the spiritual part of religion, or connected to Ouija boards and talking to the dead. They have the feeling that it is a place they don't want to go. As in 'religion I'm ok with, but Spirituality is a no-no topic'.

There is a difference between religion and spirituality. To quote someone I read recently, 'Religion is an organisation, and spirituality is an experience'. I think the major difference is that most religions believe that man is inherently flawed, that he is not as he should be, not as God expects or demands that he be, whereas the form of Spirituality that I espouse has it that we are perfect, and we are exactly as we are supposed to be, remembering of course that 'You are not your behavior'.

My spirituality is about believing that God gave us a life to live in anyway we choose to live it, and that there is no universal plan for your life, or if there is, maybe part of it is of your own making. Part of you made your plan, because part of you is God. That is really the bottom line. Many people think there is a divine path for their life that they're supposed to follow to be 'saved' if only somebody would tell them what it is. A little like a fish who has been told there is this life-giving magic stuff called water somewhere and if he could find it, all would be well and he would live for ever. Some people spend their entire life looking for the divine path, looking for signs from the almighty, messages from God pointing to the right way to live. Of course, the messages are all their own interpretation, as is everything else. I believe they are already on their divine path, as there is no way they cannot be.

* * * * * * * *

This belief opens up two possibilities. Either you have the right to do anything you want to do, or your life has all been planned out by God and there are no side roads off your life's path.

* * * * * * * *

My beliefs allow for both of these possibilities. The events in your life were known before you came here, and your soul knew them. That of course means that part of you is God. That seems like a rash statement, but then, what else do you think your soul is?

* * * * * * * *

Let's go back a step. I said that there are no divisions in eternity. I do not believe there is a division between souls. We are all equal. More significantly, we are all one. There is only one of us here. And my soul is part of God. Your soul, and my soul, and indeed everyone's soul is part of God. We, collectively, are God experiencing life, and my soul, which is part of God, did the planning for my life. Not the little things, like should I have fish for tea, but the major events and happenings in my life as I'm living it. My God and I are one. In fact there is only one entity. The collective soul of Mankind is a reflection of God, and God is a reflection of the collective soul of Mankind.

It is a massive idea, and for me a massive belief and it solves the dilemma that man has been caught in for centuries. Does mankind have free choice, or is our life already mapped out for us. In keeping with a major tenant of our talks, I believe both. What happens to me is what is supposed to happen to me because that is what my soul wanted to experience this time round.

The Self-Help Delusion

Taking this belief to the extreme, I'm saying that some souls, millions during the last century, decided to experience the torture and anguish of dying in a concentration camp, or the life as a baby in an African desert, emaciated and half eaten by flies, or perhaps to accompany the body of an articulate western child dying of cancer, and all the grief and fear that that entails.

* * * * * * * *

This is one of the major stumbling blocks, and all religions and spiritual schools have a problem with this; the seeming disparity between the 'good' and the 'bad'. And that is because there is no explanation that makes rational sense from where we are now. We are steeped in this good / bad, right / wrong thinking which we need in this existence, because everything in this world is relative. Religions fully endorse these divisions, and so have devised ideas like 'karma' to make sense of these aspects of our earthly life.

Experience – from a soul point of view - does not mean feeling every pain, every indignity, every fear, in the same way our mind does, because the soul knows that this life is a passing experience, not a statement of fact. A soul has no fear of the future, no fear of death or social rejection. It has no guilt or regret, no shame or ignorance. As we have an observer who looks on our actions in this world, so the soul observes with a benign interest, but from a very different non-worldly position. The soul does not make the acceptable / unacceptable judgments that we make to process the happenings in this existence.

Albert Einstein said:

> *"The significant problems we face cannot be solved at the same level of thinking we were at when we created them."*

Whatever the conditions and thinking that created a problem it will not be solved at that level. The thinking and beliefs that cause violence will not stop violence. It requires beliefs and thinking at a higher level to do that. Jesus, in his wisdom, gave us the commandment to 'Love your enemies, do good to those who hate you', 'turn the other cheek' etc. That is thinking at a higher level. We have created the questions as outlined above because from where we are now, it seems like a problem. Indeed, it is a problem. From where the soul is, it isn't. There are no answers using 'this world' thinking. We need to go to a higher level to make sense of it.

If that sounds like a get out, that's because we are trying to make earthly sense of un-earthly events. There are no answers at this level of thought. Mathematically, it's like trying to solving a problem with three unknown values, with only two equations. It cannot be done because there is not enough information.

* * * * * * * *

Going back a little, I'm saying that if you fight yourself out of whatever difficulties life presents, that is what you're 'supposed' to do, and if you go under because of what happens to you, that is also what you are 'supposed' to do. We cannot in fact do anything other than what we are supposed to be doing. But all that you are doing is a choice, and whatever you choose will be the way 'you' planned it to be. Be it success or failure.

Except that your soul does not think of it in terms of success or failure. If whatever happens is what is supposed to happen, how can that be considered a failure? Or even a success for that matter?

I say again, whatever we do is what we are supposed to be doing? How can it be any other way? Anything else is a fantasy that you have created in your mind because of the fear and guilt laid on you by parents or society or religion when you were young and which you were not able to protect yourself against.

This of course means that you can do anything you want in this world and all will be well with you, it's what was bound to happen, and it's not your fault. You can do entirely as you wish and there will be no retribution from God. How can there be when you have done what your soul, which is a part of God, had planned to do?

This of course gives carte-blanch for people to do as they wish to do. But remember one thing. When fear of life and death has been

The Self-Help Delusion

taken away because of these beliefs, you are left with love. Because love is what you are. And love will do no harm. Indeed, cannot do harm; to yourself or others.

Because once you realise that we are all one, you realise that hurt to another is hurt to yourself.

Ultimately of course, you cannot really hurt another because the outcome of their life in this incarnation, and yours too for that matter is not in doubt, and of course their soul has eternal life, as does yours. The trick to realise is that many promises in Holy Scripture are conditional; 'and you shall have eternal life'. (If you do what you 'should' do, and make the 'right' decisions). I believe that is more usefully read as ... 'and you do have eternal life, and this is part of it'. Your life here is part of your eternal life.

I am saying that you cannot be saved, because being saved leads you to believe that you could be unsaved. And since there is no hell for you to go to, you cannot be un-saved. As there is no heaven either, the opposite ideas of saved and unsaved have no relevance, and it's a non-question.

Time and again our culture and existence in this life lead us to create opposites to everything, because in this world, everything has opposites, everything is relative. Mankind, when he made up the religions, couldn't conceive of a system without opposites, because to his uncultured and unknowing mind, opposites were a way of life. Everything in this world is relative.

In the spirit world there are no opposites, at least, there is no reason to believe there is. There is no heaven because there is no hell. You cannot be saved because you cannot be unsaved. When you die, your higher self / spirit / soul continues to exist without a body. It doesn't go to heaven, it doesn't go to hell. It is not saved, it is not dammed. This way of seeing things, this earthly way of seeing things is simply not relevant in the spirit world. It is simply a very different way to see things.

You might ask, how do I know that it's true? And of course, I have no idea if it is true or not. Certainty is the worst of man's afflictions. Those people who are certain they're right cause the most problems in the world and the reason they cause problems is because when you are certain about something, you have no opportunity to learn. You cannot move on, because you do not accept that there is anything, the knowledge of which will change your world.

To quote a phrase 'The mind is like a parachute, it works better when it's open.' I would add to that, 'but not so open that the brains fall out'

I started this book with the attitude, 'I know nothing.' This book, and the next, are a result of an analytical approach to the human condition, and an open attitude to the spiritual world and my truth from within me; my truth notice, not the truth.

Some ideas expressed here will no doubt be new to you; but what a way to live a life, and what a way to look forward to a death. And what is the alternative? The world as we have it today which is an excellent advert for man's current beliefs and actions? What you see is what you get. Mankind has created the world from his beliefs about himself. His fears and limited understanding of what he actually is. It just follows on from there.

I said earlier that these beliefs give carte-blanch for people to do as they wish to do. And yes it does. There may be retribution in this world, but certainly not in the next.

Because if you believe all that we have spoken of and make it part of your life, then you wouldn't want to do anything that would hurt another, or do anything which was not in line with their will for themselves because these beliefs take away fear, and it is fear that causes man to behave in ways against his fellow man. And we are all one soul, part of God, and there is only one of us here.

Don't forget that when old habits kick in and you do something 'wrong', you may then realise 'that action is not representative of me in this world, and I will stop doing it'. That's OK. That action gave you an opportunity to determine what you aren't. You realise that that action is not what you really want to do in your life. Remember - to quote Conversations with God, 'Without that which I am not even that which I am is not'.

When I share these spiritual ideas about perfection, and that perfection is God's natural state, our natural state, the state of all that has been created, and the only state that he/she can be, I get exactly those resistances. As in 'All this sounds like a Pollyanna

The Self-Help Delusion

world, a cloud cuckoo land, new age feel-good stuff. That's not the way it really is'. My answer to that is, 'Why shouldn't it be feel good stuff? What is it about the way you see yourself, or God, or your life, that has you believe that it shouldn't or can't be 'Feel Good'? Perhaps you believe yourself to be unworthy, and you have picked up these feeling of unworthiness from all the people who have played a part in your life who feel themselves to be unworthy. You have taken on their truths as your own.

Earlier I said that that the world is a mirror of ourselves; that we see the world as we see ourselves. The same thing applies to every aspect of your world, including your concepts about the next one. The way you believe the next world to be is a reflection of the way you see yourself here and now.

I think that is a truly significant realisation. Many people believe that Death, Hell, Satan, the Devil, Judgment, everlasting pain and torment are actual realities in the afterlife. I mean, why would you think that? Is it about the way you see yourself that has you believe that it can't be sweetness and light in the way I'm describing it to you?

Some might think that all this sounds too good to be true. Does this mean that our alternatives sound so bad that they have to be true?

* * * * * * *

As I keep saying, we're making it all up. Let us at least make it up in a way that is useful to us.

Conclusion

This book has been about your awareness of your choices in this life on earth, and the way you have created the world as you see it. If you have acknowledged these discussions, then you will realise that this is only the first step to a fuller awareness. The question is, how do you move from the very practical aspects of your life which we have discussed in this first book and move onto the next plane; always assuming that you want to make the flight. Many people would say that there is absolutely no benefit and no logical reason why they should think about spirituality, about their higher self. Because of this they are often reluctant to think about their soul, their God, and what part they play in this cosmic game.

That's ok. You read this book because you were looking for an approach to creating a more comfortable life here, so from the word go you were prepared to read on. As a last little point I can only say; be prepared to listen, observe, grow and learn from anyone, for all people, young and old, black and white, males and females, alive or dead, have something that will move you forward if your heart is open to them, if your heart is open to what they are communicating to you. All people have something to teach you, and to assist you in demonstrating and experiencing who you are choosing to be this time round. Everyone. Why else do you think this book came into your life? Did you think it was just coincidence that we met?

* * * * * * * *

Whatever problems you did, have simply become choices which you now no longer chose.

"You see Doctor, it used to hurt when I did this and now I've stopped doing it."

Bibliography

The quotations in this book come from a series of writings. Below, I have included what to me have provided the greatest insights, presented in the most easily understood form.

Philosophy
Ken Wilber	The Spectrum of Consciousness
Carlos Castaneda	All the Don Juan series
J Krishnamurti	The Awakening of Intelligence
Tony de Mello	Awareness

Spiritual
Stephen Levine	Who dies
	A Gradual Awakening
	Healing into Life and Death
	Meetings at the edge
Neale Walsch	All the 'Conversations with God' series
Ken Keyes Jr.	Handbook to Higher Consciousness
Elisabeth Kubler-Ross	On Death and Dying
	The Wheel of Life – Autobiography
M Scott Peck	The road less travelled etc.

Psychology
Eric Berne (TA)	Transactional Analysis in Psychotherapy
	What to say after you say Hello
	Games People Play
David Gordon	Therapeutic Metaphors

Communication

Genie Z Laborde	Influencing with Integrity
Fisher Ury and Patton	Getting to Yes and Getting Past No
Deborah Tannen	Talking from 9 to 5
	You Just Don't understand
Robin Lakoff	Language and Woman's Place
Shelle Rose Charvet	Words that Change Minds

NLP

Bandler and Grinder	Frogs into Princes
	Reframing – NLP and the Transformation of Meaning
Richard Bandler	Time for a Change
	Using Your Brain for a Change
Steve Andreas	Change your Mind and Keep the Change
Anthony Robbins	Unlimited Power etc.

Business

Steven Covey	The Seven Habits of Highly Effective People
	First Things First

www.ingramcontent.com/pod-product-compliance
Lightning Source LLC
LaVergne TN
LVHW011416080426
835512LV00005B/96